PROTECTING
THE PIG

HRH Publishing
712 Nash Drive
Raleigh, North Carolina 27608

ISBN: 978-1-7348661-0-0 (print)
ISBN: 978-1-7348661-1-7(ebook)

Cover photograph by Anna Routh Barzin

Ordering Information:
Special discounts are available on quantity purchases by corporations, associations, and others. For details, contact:

Info@ProtectingThePig.com
www.ProtectingThePig.com

PROTECTING
THE PIG

How Stock Market Trends
Reveal the Way to
Grow and Preserve your Wealth

JEFF LINK

CONTENTS

Disclaimer

The contents of this book, including any references to materials or investments presented herein, do not constitute an investment recommendation. As such, this book does not contain all information that a prospective investor may desire in evaluating an investment strategy or individual investment.

Each investor must rely on his or her own examination of an investment strategy or individual investment, including the merits and risks involved in making an investment decision. Prior to making an investment decision, a prospective investor should consult his or her own counsel, accountants, and other financial professionals to evaluate the merits of an investment strategy or individual investment. Additionally, past performance of any investment strategy or individual investment referenced herein should not be relied upon as a guarantee of future performance, and no warranty of future performance is intended or implied.

This book is not intended to teach you how to manage your financial investments, but rather to teach certain investment-related concepts that may help you to become a more successful investor with the help of an investment professional.

The opinions in this book are those of the author only and are as of the date of publication. They are subject to change without notice.

Dedication

This book is dedicated to Yahweh my Elohiym and His only begotten Son, Yeshua my Lord, my Savior, my Redeemer, and my King.

> Praise ye the LORD. Praise the LORD, O my soul. While I live will I praise the LORD: I will sing praises unto my God while I have any being. Put not your trust in princes, nor in the son of man, in whom there is no help. His breath goeth forth, he returneth to his earth; in that very day his thoughts perish. Happy is he that hath the God of Jacob for his help, whose hope is in the LORD his God: Which made heaven, and earth, the sea, and all that therein is: Which keepeth truth forever: Which executeth judgement for the oppressed: Which giveth food to the hungry. The LORD looseth the prisoners: The LORD openeth the eyes of the blind: the LORD raiseth them that are bowed down: the LORD loveth the righteous: The LORD preserveth the strangers; he relieveth the fatherless and widow: but the way of the wicked he turneth upside down. The LORD shall reign forever, even thy God, O Zion, unto all generations. Praise ye the LORD.

—Psalms 146 (KJV)

Note:

All charts are available in the References section.

Also, color versions of the charts are available at
www.ProtectingThePig.com.

Special Thanks

Thank you for purchasing this book. In addition to making an investment in yourself, your purchase will make an investment in the lives of others. While living, it is my express intent to donate at least 55 percent of royalties to support charities in the state of North Carolina whose programs support primarily orphans, children with special needs, and food banks.

I also wish to thank the following people who contributed to this book. Without their help, I could not have completed this project: my wife, Julie, Book Launchers, Allen Summerford, Bradley Turlington, Claire Young, William Gupton, Pa Manneh, Bryan Yurko, Chris Peck, Christian Olmstead, David Forrest, Dianne Rogers, Tammi Rowe, Courtney Barbee, and all the individuals who shared their stories for this book, whose names will remain anonymous. You know who you are. Thank you.

CHAPTER 1

Cause and Effect

Follow the trend lines, not the headlines.

–BILL CLINTON

MALLORY WAS IN SHOCK. EIGHTEEN MONTHS EARLIER she had sold her business and invested the proceeds in the financial markets, expecting her wealth to grow. But her most recent monthly investment statement was showing a loss of 42 percent!

This is her story.

Mallory co-owned and operated a retail service business with her father in the mid-1990s. And while she was a co-owner, she managed all of the business's day-to-day operations. But six years into their partnership, Mallory and her father realized the business wouldn't support them both financially, so Mallory's father sold her his interest and retired.

Over the next six years, Mallory ran the business. She managed a staff of 30 full-time and up to 20 part-time employees depending on the season. It was common for her to work 60 to 80 hours every week, and the long hours and repetitive nature of the work began to take a toll.

In early 2007, she was approached by a consolidation company that wanted to buy her business. After a brief period of negotiations, they came to terms for a sale. It took a speedy 90 days for the entire transaction to come to pass. The whole thing happened so fast that Mallory wasn't sure what to do next. So she deposited the check at her local bank as she considered her options.

The teller suggested Mallory meet with one of the investment professionals in the bank's private client group. Since Mallory had always trusted the bank, she agreed to an initial meeting. That meeting led to several more and before long she had a plan. Even though she had profited handsomely from the sale, she didn't have enough to retire and maintain her desired lifestyle, so she continued working as a consultant for the consolidation company. Her new investment professional recommended investing 90 percent of her money in stock mutual funds and 10 percent in bond mutual funds as part of her long-term financial plan. With her consent, her money was invested in the financial markets over the next three months using a dollar-cost-averaging strategy.

Even though Mallory didn't know much about investing in financial markets, especially the stock market, she was eager to watch her wealth grow while she continued to work. She believed everything would work out well since, as she understood it, time was on her side.

But the 42 percent loss on her statement told her otherwise. Mallory lost confidence, and before long she began to make changes to her "long-term" plan to attempt to recover those losses.

Everything you just read about Mallory's story is true with one exception: Mallory isn't her real name. I chose the name Mallory because it means "unfortunate,"[1] and what I find most unfortunate about her story is I believe some of her losses were preventable. But I don't want you to take my word for it—there's proof.

Before I get into it, though, I want to acknowledge there are many financial markets available for you to invest in. They consist of stock markets, bond markets, commodities markets, currency markets, and real estate markets, to name just a few. But for purposes of this book, I will either reference a specific market by name, such as the *stock market*, or all markets in general by referring to them as the *financial markets*.

It seems most people have their own thoughts and beliefs about the stock market. Some believe stock market price movements are random, even chaotic. I have heard it said before that investing in the stock market is like gambling. And in the early years of my career, I thought that was true. But as I acquired more knowledge over the years, I came to the exact opposite conclusion: stock markets, at least over the longer term, do not tend to be random at all.

The price movements, patterns, and trends that are often observed in the stock market are relatively consistent over history. I don't suppose this should really come as any surprise. After all, major historical events encourage investors to make one of two choices: buy or sell. The culmination of this investor behavior over time helps contribute to the creation of trends. And we can use these trends to help with investment decisions, just as a business owner does.

For instance, consider sales trends. If you are a business owner selling several different products and the sales trend for one is increasing more than others, aren't you likely to invest more time, money, and resources in that product as long as you anticipate that trend will continue? Alternatively, if you expect continued declining sales in one of your services and you anticipate that trend to continue, aren't you likely to invest less time, money, and resources in that service, or even cancel it entirely?

How about economic trends? If you are a business owner and your research leads you to believe the economy is slowing and an economic contraction may be on the horizon, aren't you more likely to reduce further spending or business investment for a time? At least until you believe the contraction won't happen, or if it does, aren't you apt to wait until signs abound that a new expansion is beginning?

What about fashion trends? In retail, it is terribly important to have the latest fashions. Or let's look at technological trends. It's important to be offering a product or service that meets the current demand trend. The importance of recognizing these trends, *and when they are changing*, can be crucial to business owners' long-term success and profitability. So if successful business owners analyze sales trends, economic trends, demographic trends, and others when making decisions for their business, why not analyze financial market trends when making investment-related decisions?

To establish the foundation for other concepts presented in future chapters, I'll give you a little more background. The main index used to represent the United States stock market is the S&P 500 Index. Since it is not possible to invest directly in an index, The Vanguard Group created a stock mutual fund in 1976 called the Vanguard 500 Index Fund (symbol: VFINX) to replicate the index and allow investors to participate in its performance.

The information presented in Table 1 provides the performance returns, after fees, and expenses to an investor in this passive, index mutual fund for calendar years 1995 through 2004. I selected this particular 10-year period because it highlights both the extreme positive and negative years that an investor in the stock market is likely to encounter throughout their investing lifetime.

Table 1

	1995	1996	1997	1998	1999	2000	2001	2002	2003	2004
VFINX [2]	37.5%	22.9%	33.2%	28.6%	21.1%	-9.1%	-12.0%	-22.2%	28.1%	10.7%

After reviewing the information, do the performance returns appear random? Or do you notice an underlying trend? For this historical period there were two underlying *primary trends*. From calendar year 1995 through 1999, price rose each year forming a *rising primary trend*. From calendar year 2000 through 2002, price declined each year forming a *declining primary trend*. Then beginning in calendar year 2003, price began rising again, forming what turned out to be another rising primary trend.

Unfortunately, when viewing the information in Table 1, trends can only be observed in hindsight, which limits its value as a forecasting tool. To use the data more effectively requires looking at it from a different perspective. Since it is said a picture is worth a thousand words, the information presented in Table 1 has been reproduced in Chart 1. The squiggly line represents the price changes, and corresponding performance, for this index mutual fund over the 10-year period.

Chart 1

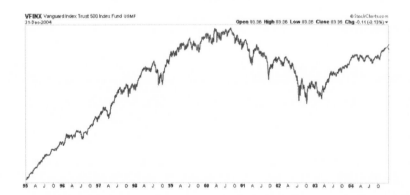

Chart courtesy of Stockcharts.com

When you look at the information from this point of view, the *general* price movement, or trend, becomes easier to see. Once again, the general trend from 1995 through 1999 was up, from 2000 to 2002 it was down, and from 2003 to 2004 it was up once again. In Chart 1A, *channels* have been added to help identify the trend. A *trend channel* forms when the price of an investment rises and declines within two parallel lines over time.

Chart 1A

Chart courtesy of Stockcharts.com

The calendar year performance from Table 1 (p. 5) has been inserted under the chart to form a complete picture between trend and performance. While stock market price changes may appear random during shorter periods of time, like any given day or week, those "random" price movements tend to converge to form distinct longer-term trend channels.

I believe we can use these trend channels to help make forecasts. Reading from the example above, and others that will follow, the financial markets over the longer term tend to form one of three types of primary trends: a *rising* trend, a *declining* trend, or a *sideways* trend.

Now you may be thinking, "I see the trends for this particular time period. But the stock market has existed for a long time. How do I know you didn't just pull this period to fit an agenda? How do I know this isn't an anomaly?" That's a great question. The best way to answer it is to look at more evidence. Since the Vanguard 500 Index Fund did not come into existence until the mid-1970s, the next three charts will illustrate the S&P 500 Index itself. Once again, each calendar year's performance has been added under each chart.

Chart 1B

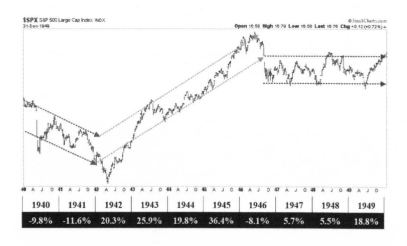

1940	1941	1942	1943	1944	1945	1946	1947	1948	1949
-9.8%	-11.6%	20.3%	25.9%	19.8%	36.4%	-8.1%	5.7%	5.5%	18.8%

Chart courtesy of Stockcharts.com

Chart 1B shows the price history for the decade of the 1940s. Beginning from the left-hand side of the chart and moving to the right, you will notice the following:

- The decade began with a *declining primary trend* that resulted in negative performance returns for calendar years 1940 and 1941.

- Beginning in 1942, the trend changed and became a *rising primary trend* that resulted in positive performance returns for calendar years 1942 through 1945.

- In 1946, the trend changed and became a *sideways primary trend* that resulted in mixed returns from 1946 through 1949.

Sideways trends may be what gives some people the impression of randomness in the stock market. When these trends occur, they may consist of alternating performance from year to year, where a positive calendar year is followed by a negative calendar year and so on. But historically speaking, this type of trend occurs less frequently than the other two.

Chart 1C

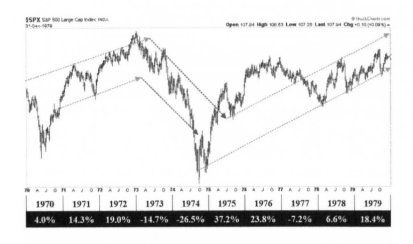

Chart courtesy of Stockcharts.com

Chart 1C shows the price history for the 1970s. Beginning from the left-hand side of the chart and moving to the right, you will notice the following:

- The first three years of the decade formed a *rising primary trend* that resulted in positive performance returns for calendar years 1970 through 1972.

- Beginning in 1973, the trend changed and became a *declining primary trend* that resulted in negative performance returns for calendar years 1973 and 1974.

- At the end of 1974 the trend changed and became a *rising primary trend* that resulted in mostly positive returns from 1975 through 1979.

Chart 1D

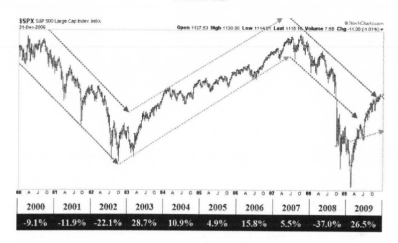

Chart courtesy of Stockcharts.com

Chart 1D shows the price history for the decade of the 2000s, which includes the year when Mallory sold her business and invested her sale proceeds. Beginning from the left-hand side of the chart and moving to the right:

- The decade began with a *declining primary trend* that resulted in negative performance returns for calendar years 2000 through 2002.

- Beginning in 2003, the trend changed and became a *rising primary trend* that resulted in positive performance returns for calendar years 2003 through 2007.

- In 2008, the trend changed and became a *declining*

primary trend that resulted in negative performance returns for that calendar year.

- In 2009, the trend changed once again, becoming a new *rising primary trend*.

So having reviewed over 40 years of stock market history, would you agree that stock markets, at least over the longer-term, do not tend to move in random, chaotic patterns?

I hope you can now see why I believe it is so important to attempt to identify the trend of each financial market you choose to invest in. If you can identify the primary trend it may help you make more informed, and hopefully profitable, investment decisions. Remember, the trend of the major stock indexes, like the S&P 500 Index, may set the trend for many other publicly listed stocks. As it rises or declines, the others tend to follow.

Now do past trends guarantee the same future trends? Unfortunately, no. But with almost a hundred years of historical evidence spanning depressions, world wars, political and social change, technological innovation, and more, do you believe these trends are likely to simply disappear and become of no effect?

I do not.

KEY TAKEAWAY

Which came first, the chicken or the egg; the trend or the return? After reviewing the historical evidence, it appears the primary trend is the cause and the return is the effect.

Returning to Mallory's story, even though she experienced seasonal trends in her business that caused her to change her staffing, she didn't realize there were financial market trends she needed to be aware of. If she had, she may have made other investment decisions that could have resulted in a different financial outcome.

CHAPTER 2

The "Blue Line"

The only constant in life is change.

−Heraclitus

AFTER READING THE PREVIOUS CHAPTER AND OBSERVING the historical evidence on trends, you may have another question: "How can you tell when the trend may be changing?" That is a great question, because one of the potential benefits of using trends is to attempt to recognize a changing trend as early as possible.

One way to identify potential changes (or turning points) is by using moving averages. According to Investopedia[2], a moving average is "an indicator used in technical analysis that helps smooth out price action by filtering out the 'noise' from random short-term price fluctuations. It is a trend-following, or lagging, indicator because it is based on past prices."

A moving average is based on the past price activity of a publicly-traded investment. It can be created for any number of time periods with the only limitation being how long the investment has been trading on a public exchange. Some common time periods used with moving averages include the

5-day, 20-day, 50-day, 100-day, 150-day, and 200-day moving average. One of my favorite attributes of a moving average is it is absolute: it consists only of itself, based on past price history. A moving average can be generated through services available through StockCharts.com and Slickcharts.com, to name just two among many.

Chart 1A from the previous chapter has been reproduced as Chart 2A to incorporate a specific moving average. The moving average in this chart is represented by the wavy solid line located inside the trend channels. On my computer screen, the color of this specific moving average happens to be blue. I will refer to it hereafter as the "Blue Line" and show how it can be used as a reference point to help warn when the trend may be changing.

Chart 2A

Chart courtesy of Stockcharts.com

Starting from the left in calendar year 1995 and ending in 2000 as you move to the right, you may notice a very interesting pattern. When the S&P 500 Index is experiencing a rising trend, its price tends to remain *above* the Blue Line.

Then from late 2000 into early 2003, you may notice another very interesting pattern. When experiencing a declining trend its price tends to remain *below* the Blue Line.

Then from early 2003 through 2004, you will notice once again price rose above and *remained* above the Blue Line during what turned out to be a new rising trend.

Let's look at the other decades introduced in the previous lesson once again to see if there is historical consistency with this pattern. Let's begin by incorporating the Blue Line into Chart 1B from the previous chapter, reproduced here as Chart 2B.

Chart 2B

Chart courtesy of Stockcharts.com

Starting on the left in calendar year 1940 and ending on the
right in early 1942, you will notice the S&P 500 Index's price
remained *below* the Blue Line during most of the declining
trend. Then from early 1942 until mid-1946, its price remained *above* the Blue Line during the rising trend. Then from
mid-1946 through 1949, its price oscillated through the Blue
Line during a sideways trend. So far, so good.

Next, let's look at the decade of the 1970s. Chart 1C from the
previous chapter is reproduced here as Chart 2C.

Chart 2C

Chart courtesy of Stockcharts.com

Starting on the left in calendar year 1970, the S&P 500 Index's
price remained *below* the Blue Line during a declining trend
that previously began in early 1969. Then from mid-1970
through 1972, its price remained *above* the Blue Line during
most of the rising trend. Then from early 1973 through 1974,

its price remained *below* the Blue Line during the declining trend. Then from early 1975 through 1976, its price remained *above* the Blue Line during the rising trend. During 1977, its price fell below the Blue Line during what I call a channel correction, a concept that will be explained further in Chapter 5. Finally, its price remained above the Blue Line, albeit in somewhat choppy form, during a rising trend from 1978 through 1979.

Next, let's look once again at the decade of the 2000s. Chart 1D from the previous chapter is reproduced here as Chart 2D.

Chart 2D

Chart courtesy of Stockcharts.com

Starting on the left in calendar year 2000 and ending in early 2003, the S&P 500 Index's price remained *below* the Blue Line during the declining trend. Then from early 2003 through 2007, its price remained *above* the Blue Line during the rising trend. Then from early 2008 into early 2009, its price remained *below* the Blue Line during a declining trend. Then by mid-2009, its price rose above the Blue Line once again during what became a new rising trend.

So if we use history as a guide, certain characteristics, or patterns, tend to accompany the interaction between price and the Blue Line during different trends. Being aware of these characteristics may help us identify when the trend may be changing.

If you would like to view the primary trends for the decades not included in this chapter, please visit www.ProtectingThePig. com.

KEY TAKEAWAY

Because there will always be a subjective aspect to identifying trends, adding an objective aspect like the Blue Line can help act as a second witness to the process. This may help improve the odds of correctly identifying potential turning points in the trend.

Returning to Mallory's story, shortly after her sale proceeds became fully invested, the price of the S&P 500 Index declined below and remained below its Blue Line. Knowledge of this historical pattern may have helped alert her to potential dangers ahead. This will be illustrated further in Chapter 6.

CHAPTER 3

When Conventional Investment Wisdom Isn't Wisdom

The only way to get ahead is to
find errors in conventional wisdom.

–LARRY ELLISON

IN THE PREVIOUS CHAPTERS, YOU HAVE VIEWED changing stock market trends within different decades in history. And even though trends are not crystal balls and cannot predict what *will* happen in the future, they may help you extrapolate what to *expect* in the future. And if stock market trends are new to you, let me share a few of their potential benefits (assuming the primary trend can be identified accurately).

For instance, if you are in possession of a large amount of money, such as $500,000 or even $1 million, and want to invest a portion (or even all of it) in the stock market, the trend may help you identify a preferred entry point to make your purchase. (We'll discuss this concept further in Chapter 10.) If you already have money invested in the stock market, the trend may help identify potential exit points to sell some, if not all of your stock investments, to attempt to reduce your investment risk. (We'll discuss a sell process in more detail in Chapter 6.)

In the absence of trends, you might rely on conventional investment wisdom to guide your investment decisions throughout your life. But once you learn about trends, does conventional investment wisdom even seem like wisdom at all?

CONVENTIONAL INVESTMENT WISDOM

Conventional investment wisdom says when you invest in the stock market, you should be willing to take more investment risk when you are younger because you have time to recover when stock markets decline. And alternatively, you should take less investment risk when you are older because you do not have time to recover from those declines. But following this wisdom may lead to a dilemma.

THE INVESTOR'S DILEMMA

If you take too much investment risk with your money, you may suffer investment loss regardless of your age. And depending on where those losses occur during your saving years, you may not accumulate enough money to achieve a work-optional lifestyle.

Alternatively, if you take too little investment risk with your money, you may not earn enough gain. And if you are retired and live long enough, you may outlive your money.

So consider conventional investment wisdom from the perspective of your two life phases: Your savings, or pre-retirement phase, and your spending, or retirement phase. What are some of the potential drawbacks of following conventional investment wisdom during these phases of life?

Your *Saving* Phase

Your saving phase may span 30 years or more, and if you are like some people, it may begin in your 20s or 30s and continue into your 60s. During this phase, your investment mindset tends to be growth-oriented for a couple reasons.

First, you are working and receiving a paycheck. Since you may not need to rely on your investments for many years, you may be willing to tolerate potential investment loss in exchange for higher potential investment gains. And second, you may be able to recover from investment losses more quickly during this phase by saving and adding more money to your investments when stock markets decline. So you might not believe your choice of investment strategy is crucial during this phase of your life.

But consider this: When you are younger, you may not have much wealth while you are in the process of accumulating it. So even taking higher risk might not reward you with a significant gain in terms of *dollars* earned. And if the stock market trend is declining, just because you can "afford" to take risk, should you? If the trends suggest a declining stock market is taking place, wouldn't you prefer to be more conservative with your investments at that time and attempt to preserve your wealth, at least until the declining trend changes?

Your *Spending* Phase

Like your saving phase, your spending phase may span a similar number of years. If you are in your 50s or 60s when you retire from the workforce, you may need your wealth to provide for you into your 80s or even your 90s! During this phase, your investment mindset may tilt towards being more conservative for a couple of reasons.

Once you hit retirement age, you might not be getting a paycheck anymore. You may receive some income through social security, or in rarer cases, a company pension. But the amount you might receive likely pales in comparison to the paycheck you walked away from. At this stage, you are relying on your investments to provide for your remaining lifetime income needs, so you may be less willing to tolerate potential investment loss in exchange for higher potential investment gain. And second, you may not be able to recover from investment loss because you are unable to save and add more money to your investments when stock markets decline. As a result, your choice of investment strategy may be crucial during this phase of your life.

But consider this. When you are older, you likely have more wealth than ever before in your life. So taking *selective* risk could result in a significant gain in terms of *dollars* earned if you're successful. And even if you are "older," you might still want to take a risk if the trends are rising. While prevailing trends are rising, you might prefer to be more growth-oriented with your investments, regardless of your age.

THE ERROR OF CONVENTIONAL INVESTMENT WISDOM

I believe an error with conventional investment wisdom is it focuses the spotlight on the wrong factor—*you*—instead of where it belongs—the *trend*. The primary trend is the constant, not you. Sometimes a change in perspective is necessary to gain clarity. I'll provide two hypothetical examples using conventional age-based investing logic to help illustrate my point.

Example #1: "Based on your age..."

For this example, consider three people whom I will refer to as Sarah, Rebecca, and Rachel. They don't know each other but all three work with the same investment professional. And on their respective 45th birthdays, they each hold a meeting with their investment professional to discuss investment changes due to recent stock market gains. All three are concerned about potential stock market declines, and they each want to know if they should make any changes to their investments. Their professional responds to their question using conventional investment wisdom.

During the first meeting with Sarah, she tells her, "*Based on your age, you should continue to be growth-oriented and keep*

*more of your money invested in the stock market because you are
still young and have time on your side to recover from any stock
market declines."*

When she meets with Rebecca, she tells her the same thing she
told Sarah. And when she meets with Rachel, she tells her the
same thing as Rebecca.

While all meetings were held during years when Sarah,
Rebecca, and Rachel turned 45, they all took place during
different calendar years. Suppose Sarah's meeting took place
during 1995, Rebecca's in 2000, and Rachel's in 2005. Please
refer to Table 3, which shows the calendar year performance
for the S&P 500 Index[3] from 1990 through 2009.

Table 3

1990	1991	1992	1993	1994	1995	1996	1997	1998	1999
-3.1%	30.5%	7.6%	10.1%	1.3%	37.6%	23.0%	33.4%	28.6%	21.0%

2000	2001	2002	2003	2004	2005	2006	2007	2008	2009
-9.1%	-11.9%	-22.1%	28.7%	10.9%	4.9%	15.8%	5.5%	-37.0%	26.5%

For Sarah, over the next few years she would likely continue to
be confident as her stock investments increased in value. On
the other hand, Rebecca would likely have been discouraged—
at least over the next couple years—as her stock investments
decreased in value. And Rachel would have been confident,
at least for the next couple years, until she suffered significant
investment loss during 2008.

For Sarah, Rebecca, and Rachel, their choice of investment strategy may require being "lucky." Will the era of their saving phase of life align with a rising trend when they may be intentionally taking more risk with their investments? Or, will the era of their spending phase of life align with a declining trend shortly after they leave the workforce? Could their choice of investment strategy make a difference? That will be the topic of discussion for the next chapter.

Example #2: "Timing" Your Retirement

Two business owners, whom I will call Paul and Peter, find themselves in similar circumstances. Both own and operate companies in the same industry and have decided to sell them and retire on their 65th birthday. Both have similar financial savings and anticipate earning a similar amount of money from their company's sale. Both are in similar health with similar life expectancies and expect to maintain a similar lifestyle in their retirement years. One final similarity is unbeknownst to Paul and Peter, they both work with the same investment professional. You might expect them both to share a similar retirement experience, right?

But what if Paul turned 65 in 1990 and Peter in 1999? If they followed conventional investment wisdom with their investment decisions and without regard of the financial market trend (especially the stock market), Paul had a distinct advantage. The portion of his financial wealth invested in the stock market could have benefitted from the rising trend that lasted for most of the next decade. In fact, from 1995 through 1999, the S&P 500 Index rose over 25 percent annually (please refer to Table 3).

Peter, on the other hand, would not have fared as well. If he turned 65 in 1999, he could have been significantly disadvantaged. The portion of his money invested in the stock market could have declined significantly right out of the gate, losing over 15 percent annually within the first three years of retirement (please refer to Table 3 once again).

While Peter may have benefitted from selling his business just prior to a downturn in the economy (and the stock market), he may not have been able to benefit from it like Paul. While you don't have any control over when you are born, you do have control over the timing of when you retire. Imagine how different things could have been for Peter if his 65th birthday occurred in 2003, just four years later?

So having viewed stock market returns from the perspective of trends, does conventional investment wisdom still seem like wisdom? If you are not familiar with trends, your initial thoughts might be doubtful. After all, to some people what I'm suggesting is a very unconventional approach to investing. But consider the unconventional approach the Boston Red Sox adopted to win a World Series championship.

In 2002 the Oakland A's, a major league baseball team, lost several key players to free agency. In an attempt to rebuild their low-payroll team and make it competitive with higher-payroll teams, the A's implemented an unconventional approach. The team adopted a process pioneered by Bill James that sought to use *mathematics* to attempt to identify undervalued baseball players. This story was portrayed in the movie *Moneyball*, in which actor Brad Pitt played the role of Billy Beane, the general manager of the Oakland A's. Beane's outside-the-box thinking was summed up in a single spoken phrase: "Adapt or die." While the franchise didn't win a championship that year, its success prompted the Boston Red Sox to hire James in November 2002. Two years later, they won their first World Series championship in over 86 years.

KEY TAKEAWAYS

If you make investment decisions with you as the center of attention, conventional investment wisdom may seem wise. But this method opens the door to potential personal bias that can lead to emotional decisions. And after considering the historical evidence of trends, conventional investment wisdom begins to look like folly. Using trends can help reduce, but not eliminate, your personal biases from your investment related decisions. Remember, the trend is the constant, not you.

Returning to Mallory's story, her investment professional used conventional investment wisdom by talking about the "long-term." But where does it say you should remain fully invested over the long-term? Plenty of times in history the stock market has declined 30 percent, 40 percent, or 50 percent, sometimes over one year, sometimes over several. The timing of these declines in your investing lifetime can make a big difference. Imagine if Mallory had sold her business a year later than she did, and *then* invested the proceeds. Her outcome could have been markedly different.

CHAPTER 4

Straw, Sticks, or Bricks?

Strategy is about making choices, trade-offs.

–Michael Porter

Let's say you live in Washington, DC, and a traveler approaches you asking for the best way to get to New York City. Before answering, you ask the traveler a few pertinent questions: How quickly do you need to get there? Do you have any financial limitations? And do you need to make any stops along the way? Based on their responses, you might reply with one of the following answers.

- If they need to get there quickly and do not have any financial limitations, you might suggest the *best way* is to fly.

- If they have financial limitations but don't need to make stops along the way, you might suggest the *best way* is to travel by bus or train.

- If they are not in a hurry and need to stop along the way, you might suggest the *best way* is to travel by car.

Regardless of the traveler's choice, they will eventually arrive at their destination. However, each way will provide a *different travel experience*. The same could be said of investing, and the difference in those experiences may be of the utmost importance when investing a portion of your wealth in the stock market.

In this chapter, I will introduce three commonly used investment strategies, where each one can provide a *different investment experience* throughout your investing lifetime. I will refer to these three strategies generically as Buy & Hold,[4] Buy & Substitute,[5] and Buy & Sell.[6, 7, 8, 9] One of the three is a passive investment strategy; the other two are active investment strategies.

Buy & Hold

Buy & Hold attempts to maximize performance returns over the longer term by minimizing the buying and selling of the underlying investments. It's largely passive in nature. When an investment is purchased using this strategy, it is held for a period typically measured in years. It is important to understand the investment(s) will remain fully invested, regardless of the direction of the trend. In other words, if the trend is rising, the value of the investment(s) may rise. But if the trend is declining, the value of the investment(s) may decline.

Performance results for this strategy are generally dependent on two factors, both of which are outside of your control. The first factor is the primary trend in effect when the purchase decision is made, and the second factor is how long that trend continues thereafter.

A well-known financial company that offers many passive-indexing financial products using this strategy is Vanguard (www.vanguard.com). The financial products they offer for purchase mirror the performance returns of certain financial indexes, before fees and expenses.

Let's revisit the Vanguard 500 Index Fund from 1995 through 1999 (introduced in Chapter 1). Assume you purchased this passive index mutual fund at the beginning of 1995. As the stock market trend continued rising over the next five years, the value of your investment could have increased by over 25 percent annually!

However, once the trend changed in 2000 and began declining, the value of your investment from the high could have declined over the next three years by 15 percent annually. Yikes!

If you were to compare this strategy to one of the methods of travel in the story above, it might represent the train. On the way to its destination, the train travels along a direct route and is limited in its ability to change course during the journey.

Buy & Substitute

Buy & Substitute is a type of active investment strategy that may attempt to maximize performance returns over either the short or longer term. When an investment is purchased, it may be held for an indefinite period, and contrary to your expectation may remain fully invested. This may come as a surprise if you mistakenly believe that all investment professionals who use an active strategy will limit your investment loss by not remaining fully invested when the trend of the stock market is declining. The reason for this is simple but not necessarily straightforward.

In some cases, the difference between Buy & Hold and Buy & Substitute lies in the occasional *exchange* or *substitution* of one or more of your investments. For instance, assume you own shares of IBM stock along with other securities in your investment account. If your investment professional is using an active Buy & Substitute strategy, there may come a time when your IBM shares are sold and the proceeds are *substituted* into a different stock, like Microsoft.

Or instead of individual stocks, maybe some of your financial investments include stock mutual funds. Once again, assume you own shares in the "ABC Growth mutual fund" and there comes a time when your investment professional determines the "XYZ Growth mutual fund" is a better and more consistent performing fund. So all shares of the ABC Growth mutual fund are sold and the proceeds are *substituted* into the XYZ Growth mutual fund. What you need to understand with this strategy is the decision to make this substitution may be made *without regard for the current stock market trend*. Instead, the decision may be made solely by deciding which investment among a group or category of similar investments is more preferable.

A financial company that offers several actively managed financial products using this strategy is The Capital Group™ with its American Funds™ family of mutual funds (www.capitalgroup.com). Instead of trying to mirror the performance returns of various financial indexes, their financial products attempt to exceed the performance returns of financial benchmarks or indexes after accounting for fees and expenses.

As is often the case, this strategy tends to behave similarly to a Buy & Hold strategy. When the general trend of the stock market is rising, investments using this strategy tend to rise in price. And when the general trend of the stock market is declining, these same investments tend to decline in price as well.

It's like the bus. On the way to its destination, the bus travels along a fairly direct route but possesses some ability to adjust course compared to the train.

Buy & Sell

Like Buy & Substitute, Buy & Sell is another type of active investment strategy that may be more commonly referred to as "buy low, sell high." But unlike the other two, this one may not remain fully invested. The reason I refer to it as Buy & Sell is that sometimes it's better to sell an investment shortly after it is purchased and suffer a small loss rather than keeping it and potentially lose more. Not every investment decision will be a profitable one. The sooner that is recognized and corrective action is taken, the better.

Let's return once again to the example of the ABC Growth mutual fund. Before the fund is sold, the Buy & Sell strategy asks a different question: What should be purchased with the sale proceeds? For example, should they be invested in another similar investment? Or should they be invested in a cash equivalent investment? Consider once again the historical example of the Vanguard 500 Index mutual fund from Chapter 1. If you had reason to believe the rising stock market trend was coming to an end, you might prefer to sell the stock or stock mutual fund and invest the sales proceeds in something that won't decline if the stock market begins declining. Remember, it's called "buy low, sell high" for a reason. And while many investors seem to believe strongly in this strategy, I find some investors may mistakenly believe the Buy & Substitute strategy used by their investment professional is, in fact, Buy & Sell, leaving them more exposed to potential stock market losses.

Something else I believe you should know about a "buy low, sell high" strategy is that it may or may not include active trading. In using the term Buy & Sell, I am not necessarily referring to a trading strategy. I am referring to a risk-managed strategy. Such a strategy recognizes that, regardless of whether your personal time horizon is shorter term, intermediate term, or longer term, there may be occasions when it may not be prudent to remain fully invested.

This strategy is like the car. On the way to its destination, the car can change routes as often as necessary.

A HISTORICAL COMPARISON
(By percent)

Having differentiated these three strategies, I next want to show you how each one may perform, depending on the trend. The S&P 500 Index[10] will be used as the financial benchmark, and three different stock mutual funds will be used to represent each investment strategy. Table 4A includes the calendar years from 1995 through 1999 when the United States stock market was enjoying a strong rising price trend.

Table 4A

STRATEGY	1995	1996	1997	1998	1999
S&P 500 Index	37.6%	23.0%	33.4%	28.6%	21.0%
BUY & HOLD	37.5%	22.9%	33.2%	28.6%	21.1%
BUY & SUBSTITUTE	29.8%	14.8%	26.9%	31.8%	45.7%
BUY & SELL	11.0%	10.5%	12.4%	12.3%	13.0%

You will notice a correlation with performance returns during a rising trend between the index, Buy & Hold, and Buy & Substitute strategies during this five-year rising trend. While certain calendar years favored one over another, the returns were not materially different on average. This Buy & Sell strategy, however, while earning solid, long-term returns, underperformed the others.

Table 4B includes the calendar years from 2000 through 2002 when the United States stock market was reeling from a declining trend.

Table 4B

STRATEGY	2000	2001	2002
S&P 500 Index	-9.1%	-11.9%	-22.1%
BUY & HOLD	-9.1%	-12.0%	-22.2%
BUY & SUBSTITUTE	7.5%	-12.3%	-22.0%
BUY & SELL	6.6%	-3.5%	-4.9%

Once again, you will notice a similar correlation with performance returns during a declining trend. In fact, it's almost the exact opposite experience of the rising trend. The performance returns between the index, Buy & Hold, and Buy & Substitute strategies over this three-year declining trend were similar in two of the three years. The Buy & Sell strategy however, matched or outperformed the others.

Table 4C includes calendar year 2008, the year the stock market experienced one of the worst one-year price declines in history.

Table 4C

STRATEGY	2008
S&P 500 Index	-37.0%
BUY & HOLD	-37.0%
BUY & SUBSTITUTE	-39.1%
BUY & SELL	-13.9%

Like Table 4B, the correlation of results is very similar. And while the Buy & Sell strategy declined as well, it declined far less compared to the others. If investment losses can be limited, it presents the potential for a quicker recovery.

Remember, past performance is not indicative of future results, and this is being presented to show what is *possible*, not necessarily what is *probable*.

A HISTORICAL COMPARISON
(By time)

A prolonged investment loss means you don't just lose money, you also lose time. How much time depends, of course, on the size of your initial investment loss and your choice of strategy.

During your saving phase of life, you may have the luxury of waiting for your investments to recover. But during your spending phase, that luxury may not exist. Therefore, it is important to be familiar with how much time could pass before you might recover your wealth after a stock market decline.

Table 4D presents the performance results *in dollars* instead of percent, assuming you had $100 invested in each strategy at the end of 1999. Each successive calendar year thereafter reflects the value of the investment, net of all fees, based on the following year's performance.

Table 4D

STRATEGY	2000 (Y1)	2001 (Y2)	2002 (Y3)	2003 (Y4)	2004 (Y5)	2005 (Y6)	2006 (Y7)
S&P 500 Index	$ 90.94	$ 80.01	$ 62.29	$ 80.04	$ 88.63	$ 92.86	$ 107.39
BUY & HOLD	$ 90.94	$ 80.01	$ 62.29	$ 80.04	$ 88.63	$ 92.86	$ 107.39
BUY & SUBSTITUTE	$ 107.49	$ 94.71	$ 73.85	$ 97.54	$ 109.20	$ 124.75	$ 144.44
BUY & SELL	$ 106.61	$ 102.85	$ 97.85	$ 109.21	$ 116.80	$ 122.25	$ 134.64

What you may first notice is the passive Buy & Hold index strategy would have taken six to seven years to recover the investment loss from the declining trend; the active Buy & Substitute strategy would have taken three to four years to recover; and the active Buy & Sell strategy would have taken one to two years to recover.

Table 4E presents the results assuming you had $100 invested in each strategy at the end of 2007. Each successive calendar year thereafter reflects the value of the investment, net of all fees, based on the following year's performance.

Table 4E

STRATEGY	2008 (Y1)	2009 (Y2)	2010 (Y3)	2011 (Y4)	2012 (Y5)
S&P 500 Index	$ 62.98	$ 79.66	$ 91.54	$ 93.34	$108.11
BUY & HOLD	$ 62.98	$ 79.66	$ 91.54	$ 93.34	$108.11
BUY & SUBSTITUTE	$ 60.93	$ 81.94	$ 92.00	$ 87.50	$105.47
BUY & SELL	$ 86.08	$ 91.74	$ 96.17	$ 99.04	$103.51
BUY & SELL [8],[9]	$ 85.80	$126.38	$149.13	$144.51	$168.35

In this case, you will notice that most strategies would have recovered the investment losses within four to five years. However, depending on the Buy & Sell strategy used, the time required to recover could be less.

For this example, I added a second Buy & Sell strategy to further illustrate what is *possible*, not necessarily what is *probable*. Because its inception date was October 2003, it could not be used in Table 4D. But by *coincidence*, both Buy & Sell strategies were able to limit their investment losses by almost the same amount in 2008. Again, past performance is no guarantee of future results.

The Buy & Sell strategy happened to provide a better performance result during this declining trend, but it also provided a preferable investment experience during what may have been a stressful and fearful time for many investors. Having said that, I want to stress that I am not suggesting the Buy & Sell strategy is "the best" and should always be chosen over other strategies. This example merely highlights the results of a few investments that represent each of the three investment strategies. Had other investments been used for this illustration, the outcomes may have been different.

Maybe you're not a numbers person. Let's try a visual perspective. The annual performance returns from 1995 through 2014 have been reproduced in a line graph in Table 4F.

TABLE 4F

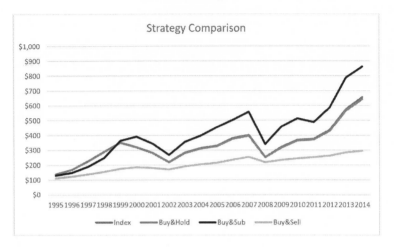

I now present you with the following question: which one of these three strategies would have been the "best" and which one would have been the "worst?"

If your answer is that the Buy & Substitute investment was clearly "the best" and the Buy & Sell investment was clearly "the worst," I believe you may be mistaken. The "best" performing strategy may have been "the worst" *depending on when the declining trends occur within your individual phase of life.* And the "worst" performing strategy may have been "the best" once again, *depending on the same.*

Some investors do not believe in "timing" the stock market. But what about the "timing" of major changes in your life, like retirement? Can being aware of the primary trend help you evaluate which strategy may be preferable depending on where you are in your phase of life? No investment strategy exists that will work to your satisfaction all the time. But as in the transportation analogy referenced above, different strategies may result in different financial experiences along the way.

KEY TAKEAWAYS

During your investing lifetime, stock market trends are likely to change. Different investment strategies will perform differently depending on the trend. So if you can successfully identify the primary trend, one strategy may be preferable over another at different points in time. Or you may prefer to choose a strategy that can adapt to those changes when they may be taking place.

Returning to Mallory's story, her investment professional recommended a Buy & Substitute strategy. Do you think Mallory would have chosen differently if she had known about the different options we talked about in this chapter?

CHAPTER 5

The "Faces" of Risk

A major lesson in risk management is that a "receding sea" is not a lucky offer of an extra piece of free beach, but the warning sign of an upcoming tsunami.

–JOS BERKEMEIJER

IN THE PREVIOUS CHAPTER, I ILLUSTRATED HOW YOU might expect different investment strategies to perform depending on the magnitude of the declining trend. I wanted to illustrate that to help stress the importance of the information presented in Table 5A.[11] I have found some investors mistakenly believe a similar price increase in the year following a previous year's price decrease will mostly offset. But that is not necessarily correct.

TABLE 5A

Digging A Hole

Small losses are easier to recover from, compared with big drops

Initial loss	Gain needed to recover
8%	8.7%
25	33
30	43
40	67
50	100

The left-hand column provides several examples of investment losses. The right-hand column provides the percent return you would need to earn after suffering the investment loss—either on an individual investment *or your entire investment portfolio*—to recover your loss.

What stands out is that a relatively small loss, like 8 percent, can be overcome with just a slightly higher investment gain of 8.7 percent. More than likely, you can tolerate a short-term, 8 percent correction, but what about a 30 percent correction? As the loss increases in magnitude, an even larger investment gain is required thereafter to recover. This table helps show why it is important to try to protect against the significant declines. For instance, if you experience a 30 percent investment loss, it will require a 43 percent gain thereafter to recover.

So returning to the trend correction of 2008, let's take a quick look at what transpired over the following year. Please refer to the information presented in Table 5B.

Table 5B

STRATEGY	2008	2009
S&P 500 Index	-37.0%	26.5%
BUY & HOLD	-37.0%	26.5%
BUY & SUBSTITUTE	-39.1%	34.5%
BUY & SELL	-13.9%	6.6%

At first glance, you may believe that the positive returns in 2009 offset much of the loss that took place during the previous year. But now you know better. For instance, had you invested $100 at the end of 2007 in the Buy & Hold strategy, the value of your investment would have dropped to $63 by the end of 2008. Then, after earning a 26.5 percent return on your ending 2008 balance, by the end of 2009 your investment would have been worth $80, still *20 percent* below your initial investment.

As you likely already know, investing in the stock market entails risk. And some risks should be acceptable to most investors, but others should not. When it comes to defining stock market risk, a common method is the degree of price volatility, specifically when prices decline. But not all price declines are the same. There are three types of price declines you are likely to experience throughout your investing lifetime. One is relatively harmless and happens more frequently. One is cause for concern and happens less frequently. And one is downright terrifying and happens infrequently. These three declines, respectively, are called a price correction, a channel correction, and a trend correction, and I will use the Dow Jones Industrial Average (DJIA)[12] to show you what they might look like.

Price Correction

A *price correction* consists of a relatively short-lived decline in the price of an investment. After the price decline comes to an end, the price typically recovers and rises higher. Chart 5A illustrates what this tends to look like during a rising trend using the DJIA from 1950 through 1955 in relation to its Blue Line.

CHART 5A

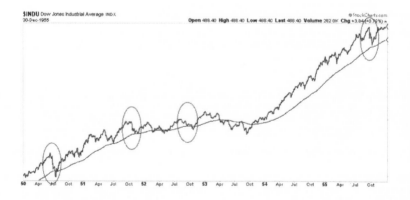

Chart courtesy of Stockcharts.com

You may notice the price of the DJIA tended to decline to its Blue Line on price corrections before "bouncing" off it and rising higher over the next few months. The four red circles highlight some of the short-term price corrections that took place during this five-year rising trend. With price corrections, the decline tends to be relatively shallow and short lived. Beginning with the left red circle and moving to the right, the four highlighted price corrections amounted to approximately -11 percent, -5 percent, -6 percent, and -9 percent. In all cases, the price rose higher shortly thereafter, and for most investors, these price corrections are likely tolerable.

Channel Correction

A *channel correction* may cause more concern due to the price decline being more significant and lasting longer than a price correction. When a channel correction occurs, a new price channel tends to form below the previous one. In Chart 5B, you will notice prices broke down from a higher trend channel (labeled "A") and fell back into the previous trend channel (labeled "B").

CHART 5B

Chart courtesy of Stockcharts.com

When this channel correction took place in 1966, prices declined 20 percent from the top of the higher channel to the bottom of the previous channel. Prices eventually recovered to their previous highs but in this instance, it took two years of waiting.

Trend Correction

A *trend correction* is, in my opinion, the greatest risk to *every* investor in the stock market. Historically speaking, these may only last from one to three years but they tend to experience *significant* price declines. The late Richard Russell, founder of Dow Theory Letters, often said that such trend corrections tend to retrace one-third to two-thirds of the previous price advance.

For instance, from January 1983 to March 2000, the DJIA rose from 1,035 to 11,600. It declined to 7,200 by October 2002. *In other words, within three years, the Dow Jones Industrial Average lost 68 percent of the gains that took 17 years to accumulate.* Stop reading for a minute and let that sink in. In another example, Chart 5C illustrates the worst trend change in history, which preceded what we now call the Great Depression.

CHART 5C

Chart courtesy of Stockcharts.com

From the highest price in 1929 to the lowest price in June 1932, the DJIA declined by 87 percent. You will also notice that price remained below the Blue Line during the nearly three-year decline.

Fortunately for investors, the stock market rises far more often than it declines. And as mentioned before, trend corrections tend to happen infrequently. But what if another happens within your investing lifetime? Wouldn't it be convenient if there was a way to try and recognize when one may be about to take place? You could take proactive and preventive action that may help limit your investment loss.

I believe there is a way to recognize these trend corrections, and that is the topic of discussion for the next chapter.

KEY TAKEAWAYS

Not all price corrections are the same. Some are minor, occur frequently, and are relatively harmless. Others can be major, occur infrequently, and can be extremely harmful. Using reference points, like the Blue Line or trend channels, may help differentiate between them to help set your future expectations for what proactive investment actions, if any, you might decide to take.

Returning to Mallory's story, she became fully invested in her stock mutual funds right before a trend correction began. Her choice of investment strategy did not use a sell process to make changes once the trend changed. In the next chapter, I will show you one example of a sell process that might have helped her limit some of her investment loss.

CHAPTER 6

When Selling May Be Your Best Option

Rule No. 1: Never lose money.
Rule No. 2: Never forget Rule No. 1.

—WARREN BUFFETT

IN CHAPTER 1, I MADE A BOLD STATEMENT. NOT ONLY did I say that I believed some of Mallory's losses were preventable but I also said there was proof. In this chapter, I'll show you what I meant by that statement.

In the previous chapters, I have been laying a foundation. I illustrated three types of price "corrections" and some of their differentiating characteristics. Now I want to take these concepts deeper and prove why I believe trends could make a significant difference in your investment success.

In Chapter 4, I showed you how a risk-managed investment strategy may help limit losses when stock markets decline, especially during a trend correction. But before I go into it, I want to share an analogy to help you with this concept.

Speed limit signs are posted along roadways to provide notice

of the maximum safe travel speed under ideal weather conditions. But in some cases, they do not specify a minimum speed limit.

Let's assume you are on a road trip. As you travel along the highway you glance down at your odometer and notice you are traveling at 75 MPH. There are storm clouds forming on the horizon. Before long, the wind starts to pick up and shortly thereafter it starts sprinkling. The weather conditions are beginning to change but there may not yet be a cause to slow down. Then the rain begins to come down harder and faster and your visibility diminishes. As road conditions deteriorate, you decide it's a good idea to slow down to avoid a potential accident. Even though the posted speed limit is 75 MPH, you may find yourself driving at 55 MPH. And if the storm gets bad, you may decide to pull off to the side of the road, stopping altogether, until the storm passes. When travel conditions become favorable again, you pull back on the road and resume your trip, traveling at 75 MPH.

The varying types of "storms" you may encounter in stock market investing were presented in the last chapter. And for the most part, the one storm that might cause you to want to pull over to the side of the road is a trend correction. In order to do so, you need to use an investment strategy that uses some type of *sell process*.

A sell process is a rules-based method that can help identify when you may be better off selling one or more of your stock investments and holding the proceeds in cash or cash-equivalent investments. This could help limit potential investment loss when stock markets are declining. You may be familiar with the saying "cash is an asset class." And while many investors believe this, few seem to pursue a strategy that uses it.

On October 12, 2016, CNBC interviewed Jim Cramer, the host of *Mad Money*. In the interview, the CNBC host said, "The biggest mistake Jim Cramer sees investors make is that many think they are supposed to be fully invested at all times. Heck, even some money managers have told him they are supposed to have all their money in stocks. This is complete nonsense! Having cash on hand when a market correction occurs is the key to protecting a portfolio. Sometimes the market will stink, and there is nothing to do but just sit in cash."

> *Cramer went on to say, "In fact, one of the chief reasons that I outperformed pretty much every manager in the business during my 14-year run as a professional money manager is that there were substantial blocks of time when I was largely in cash."*

In 2010, a book about the subprime mortgage crisis of 2008 was published. *The Big Short* was based on the life of Michael Burry, the founder of the hedge fund Scion Capital, which he ran from calendar years 2000 through 2008. One of my favorite quotes from him is, "*It is ludicrous to believe that asset bubbles can only be recognized in hindsight.*" I tend to agree.

Returning to the point of this chapter, if I told you that some of history's most significant stock market declines shared a similar *pattern*, would you believe me? What if you could look for this pattern to try to identify when a financial storm may be looming on the horizon so you can take proactive measures in hopes of limiting potential loss? I will show you what I am referring to, and in doing so, attempt to prove my previous statement.

I'll show you the first example in layers. Chart 6A illustrates the price changes in the S&P 500 Index beginning in calendar year 1965 and ending in 1970.

CHART 6A

Chart courtesy of Stockcharts.com

In Chart 6B, the Blue Line is added to help act as a reference point.

CHART 6B

Chart courtesy of Stockcharts.com

In Chart 6C, the trend channel is identified using technical analysis, based on past price changes even before 1965. I have narrowed this chart down to help focus your attention on what I believe is most important. The trend channel, identified by the two horizontal dashed lines, is drawn in based on experience. There are no guarantees that what I believe is the primary channel is in fact correct. Experience helps narrow down the possibilities, but one can never be certain the trend channel is correctly identified. That is why the Blue Line can come in handy as a second witness.

CHART 6C

Chart courtesy of Stockcharts.com

CHART 6D

Chart courtesy of Stockcharts.com

In 1969, the index broke through the Blue Line, as well as the bottom of the trend channel. Chart 6D illustrates the three phases of a sell process I follow that may help identify the early stages of a trend correction.

When the index dropped below the Blue Line by at least 5 percent, that can be interpreted as Phase 1, a *warning* that the trend may be changing. After a brief price rally, if the investment fails to rise back above the Blue Line, that can be interpreted as Phase 2, *failure*. In other words, price has *failed* to rise above and remain above the Blue Line. Depending on what other technical indicators may be suggesting, this may be where you would want to either sell half of the investment or add a protective hedge, if possible.

If the investment declines to a new price low, it may rally one more time back up to the bottom of the Blue Line, or the trend channel. If it does not exceed the Blue Line on a second try, that can be interpreted as Phase 3, *confirmation*. I believe the market is *confirming* the previous failure and further losses are possible. As it turned out, the index eventually declined 28 percent from Phase 3. In my opinion, if a trend correction is likely, your best option may be to sell, or hedge, your remaining investments to attempt to limit further investment loss, should they occur. (Protective hedges will be discussed in the next chapter.)

So that was 1969. Let's look at another example. I've walked you through the steps in the prior example so I will only show you the complete picture for the remaining examples. Chart

6E illustrates the trend channel for the S&P 500 Index for calendar years 1998 through 2002. At first glance, you may notice the pattern was essentially the same. Phase 1 occurred when the index initially declined through the Blue Line and the bottom of the trend channel. Phase 2 occurred with the price rally that failed to rise back above the Blue Line and the trend channel. And Phase 3 occurred when the index could not rise back above the Blue Line or the trend channel a second time.

CHART 6E

Chart courtesy of Stockcharts.com

What is important to observe is from the time the price first declined below the Blue Line until the decline neared an end in October of 2002, the index declined in price by 46 percent.

Next, let's look at what happened shortly after Mallory fully invested her money in the stock market in late 2007.

CHART 6F

Chart courtesy of Stockcharts.com

In Chart 6F, Mallory became fully invested in her stock mutual funds where "X" marks the spot. You may notice that at that time, the index was in a rising trend. However, shortly thereafter, price dropped below the Blue Line by more than 5 percent, as well as the bottom of the trend channel (Phase 1). The index experienced a short price rally back up to both the Blue Line and the bottom of the trend channel but failed to exceed either (Phase 2). Price declined to a new low and on the rally, thereafter, failed to reach the Blue Line (Phase 3). Then the market crashed.

From the time the index broke down through the trend channel and the Blue Line until the price decline came to an end, the stock market suffered an excruciating loss of 52 percent. It's important to keep in mind that this loss was from the Blue Line—not the price "high."

What I have just showed you is a pattern that coincided with significant stock market price declines. And even though the *reasons* attributed to the decline were all different, the *pattern* was almost the same in every instance. (On a side note, while I have not illustrated it in this book directly, you may find it interesting that the stock market crash that coincided with the Great Depression followed this same pattern).

Now I want to stress a *very* important point. When this pattern manifests, it does not predict the potential *magnitude* of price decline that may follow thereafter or whether or not a price decline will follow at all! What I believe it suggests is that the risk of investment loss may be high. As a profit-seeking investor, you must decide if you want to remain fully invested and hope for the best or take proactive action to ensure you are prepared for the worst.

While some companies suggest you remain fully invested and ride through the storm, after reviewing these trend corrections and the potential losses that may accompany them, the question to ask is who would want to?

KEY TAKEAWAYS

Some investment strategies attempt to manage risk through an asset allocation decision. However, without a sell process, the portion invested in the stock market always remains at risk so I don't believe this can be termed managing risk. I believe a sell process is a better option.

Few people, if any, will be fortunate enough to sell out at a price "top" and buy back in at the price "bottom," but I do not believe that tactic is necessary either. If you can use some type of sell process to limit your losses, it may create future investment opportunities that may not be available otherwise.

Back to Mallory: Imagine if she had chosen a risk-managed investment strategy like the one illustrated in Chapter 4. Had she recognized the potential for a trend correction rising, she may have been able to limit her investment loss.

CHAPTER 7

Two-Dimensional Investing

Minimizing downside risk while
maximizing the upside is a powerful concept.

–MOHNISH PABRAI

WHEN STOCK MARKET PRICES ARE RISING, SOME
investors may cave to a fear of missing out on future potential
returns and remain fully invested. This mindset has been
reinforced over the years by the marketing messages of certain
financial institutions and investment professionals alike.
But this mindset also works in reverse—by remaining fully
invested, investors will participate in losses when stock market
prices are declining. I call this one-dimensional investing.
Who says you can't remain fully invested *and* protect some of
your stock market wealth when stock markets decline?

In the previous chapter, I introduced a concept called a sell
process or sell discipline. The idea behind such a process
is to attempt to identify when you may be better off selling
one, or a number, of your stock investments in favor of cash
equivalents, to attempt to preserve your wealth when the stock
market is declining. In this chapter, I want to take this concept

further and will use the following example to do so.

Let's assume your total stock market wealth is $100 and is invested in a single exchange-traded fund—the SPDR S&P 500 ETF (symbol: SPY). This ETF mirrors the performance of the S&P 500 Index, before fees and expenses. If the stock market rises, you would expect your $100 to rise as well. Likewise, if it declines, you would expect your $100 to decline. Now let's say you believe the stock market may be at risk of a decline and you want to protect some of your stock market wealth. What are your options?

Based on the information presented in the previous chapter, you might use a sell process to sell a portion of your investment. For instance, you might sell $25 of SPY, leaving you with $75 invested in SPY and $25 in cash. By taking this action, you have reduced your risk by 25 percent. Unfortunately, you still have 75 percent of your stock market wealth at risk of decline. And if your investment is owned in a taxable account and has appreciated, unrealized gains, additional sales could result in realized taxable gains.

A second option uses what I call two-dimensional investing. With two-dimensional investing you afford yourself the opportunity to remain fully invested but with reduced risk. There are several financial tools that can be used to accomplish this but for purposes of this book, I will refer to one specific investment called an inverse ETF. An inverse ETF is an "exchange-traded fund constructed by using various derivatives to profit from a decline in the value of an underlying benchmark."[13] These investments are like shorting, or in more simple terms, selling high and buying low. This concept is advanced, but I believe it is important for you to know.

Before I provide you with a numerical example, let's turn back time once again and look at a visual example. In calendar year 2008, the S&P 500 Index declined significantly from early September until late November. Please refer to Chart 7A that illustrates the sharp decline.

CHART 7A

Chart courtesy of Stockcharts.com

The price of the SPY ETF declined over 40 percent from early June to late November 2008. However, even though the price of this particular investment was declining, a different investment was rising. In Chart 7B, you will find an inverse ETF, called the ProShares Short S&P 500 ETF (symbol: SH). As you can see, while the price of SPY was declining, the price of SH was rising!

CHART 7B

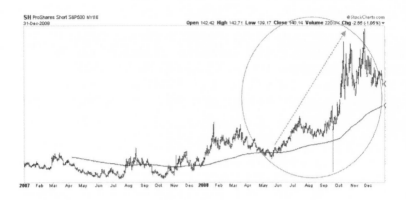

Chart courtesy of Stockcharts.com

To help you understand how these investments may be used to help protect your stock market wealth when stock market prices are declining, think about the original $100 investment in SPY in terms of four $25 increments.

By selling $25 of SPY and purchasing $25 of SH, the $25 in SH predominately (but not completely) offsets one of the other three $25 remaining in SPY. If your investment in SPY declines after your purchase of SH, your stock market wealth could be protected by approximately 50 percent–even though you only purchased 25 percent of the inverse ETF.

I believe this can be an effective way to reduce investment risk, especially when your stock investments are in taxable accounts. By selling less of SPY (in this example), you might limit any potential unrealized taxable gains; you would continue to remain fully invested and you could have reduced your risk by half. By adding inverse ETFs to your investment arsenal, I believe you create the opportunity for what I call two-dimensional investing. Just because the stock market may be declining doesn't mean all your stock investments have to decline as well.

Chart 7C provides another example using a different investment: The SPDR Dow Jones Industrial Average ETF (symbol: DIA). This ETF mirrors the performance of the Dow Jones Industrial Average, before fees and expenses. As you can see, a sharp price decline of approximately 13 percent took place during August 2015. Fortunately, it proved short-lived and a couple months later, the price recovered.

CHART 7C

Chart courtesy of Stockcharts.com

CHART 7D

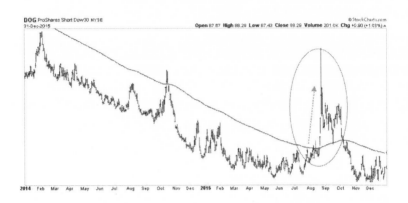

Chart courtesy of Stockcharts.com

In Chart 7D, you will find the inverse ETF, called the ProShares Short Dow 30 ETF (symbol: DOG). Like the example provided above, while the price of DIA was declining, the price of DOG was rising.

While these investments can be used in a speculative manner to try to profit when stock markets decline, that is not how I am presenting them in this chapter. I believe they can be helpful and effective investments to protect a portion of your stock investments when used with a disciplined sell process. If you are wondering when such investments should be sold after they are purchased, I am sorry to say that I might have to write another book to provide a satisfactory answer.

Given the complex nature of these investments, I do not believe they should be used if the potential risks are not fully understood. I simply want to present them as an alternative to cash or cash equivalents and show how they might help reduce your stock market risk. If you are interested in learning more about these particular inverse ETFs, please visit www. proshares.com.

KEY TAKEAWAYS

When the stock market experiences a price decline, that doesn't mean every one of your stock investments has to decline as well. Inverse ETFs can be used as an effective protective hedge to reduce some of your investment risk. Of course, the effectiveness will at least partly depend on the types of stock investments your wealth is invested in.

As for Mallory, inverse ETFs were relatively new in 2007. So more than likely, had she chosen a Buy & Sell strategy, cash or cash equivalents might have been her primary means of reducing risk at that time.

CHAPTER 8

If You Don't Learn From the Past, You're Likely to Repeat It

What determines your wealth is not how much you make
but how much you keep of what you make.

–DAVID BACH

I ASSUME YOU ARE READING THIS BOOK BECAUSE YOU
are either already wealthy or are in the process of accumulating
wealth. You may be the owner of a successful business. You
may be in possession of appreciated real estate. You may have
appreciated stock from a successful initial public offering
(IPO). You may have a growing 401(k) plan to which you have
been contributing for years. Or you may expect to receive a
family inheritance in the future. Regardless of the source, a day
may come when you monetize your wealth. Maybe you will
sell your business, or your real estate, or leave the workforce
and roll over your 401(k). If that day comes, you will have to
choose how to reinvest it. And if your choice is not aligned
with the trend, it may impact whether you remain wealthy.

This is a good time to briefly recap several of the pertinent
concepts presented in the first six chapters. First, trends exist in

the financial markets. Second, these trends change over time. Third, the performance returns for some investment strategies are more dependent on the direction of the prevailing trend than others. Fourth, being unaware of trends, especially a trend correction, may result in significant financial loss. And fifth, familiarity with the trend patterns that have preceded some of history's more significant stock market declines may help you protect some of your wealth from significant loss by using a sell process.

While I was writing this book, I had the privilege of meeting many successful people, all of whom were more than happy to share their stories. And while I am forever grateful to them all, I will share three of their stories here, and I will call these individuals David, William, and Martin.

All three created their wealth through their businesses and, like Mallory, they all benefitted from successful and profitable sales. Each one chose to invest a portion of their sale proceeds in the stock market using one of the investment strategies introduced in Chapter 4.

You may guess that one of these people chose Buy & Hold, one chose Buy & Substitute, and one chose Buy & Sell. Who do you believe might continue to both grow and preserve their wealth over the coming years?

I'll begin with David.

David's Story

David owned and operated two companies during his working lifetime. He started the first in 1992 out of his house and grew it to where it eventually employed 18 full-time employees. After many years of frustration and stress, he sold it in 2005 for little profit.

Upon identifying what he believed was a better opportunity, he started his second company in 2007. He applied all the valuable experience he had accumulated through his previous endeavor and turned this business into a smashing success. In 2018, he deposited a seven-figure check from the sale. After 26 years of struggle, stress, hard work, and perseverance, David and his family were financially wealthy.

David's Decision

For the first time in his life, David had more money than he knew what to do with. Since he had not previously worked with an investment professional during his working years, he wasn't sure what to do or who to turn to.

So he decided to invest his money on his own. David began conservatively, investing approximately 80 percent of his money in short-term Certificates of Deposit (CDs)[14] at various banks in his area. In doing so, he shared Mallory's experience. Every bank teller tried to introduce him to their bank's private client group. But unlike Mallory, he said no. He invested the other 20 percent in a stock index mutual fund through Vanguard.

David's Investment Strategy and Outlook

Based on what you read in Chapter 4, you may recognize that whether knowingly or unknowingly, David chose a Buy & Hold investment strategy. In other words, his future investment performance for all investments will be 100 percent dependent on trends, unless he decides to make a change.

For instance, as long as he continues to invest in short-term CDs, the interest he earns will be dependent on the trend in short-term interest rates as dictated by the Federal Reserve. If rates remain low, the amount of interest he earns will be low. Should the trend in rates rise, his interest payments are likely to rise as well.

Regarding his stock investment, if the stock market trend continues as a rising trend after his purchase, he is likely to enjoy financial gain. But if, or when, the trend changes in the future and begins declining, he may suffer financial loss. Remember, a Buy & Hold strategy is a reactive, not proactive strategy. I like to think of it as an airplane flying on autopilot. If a storm appears on the horizon and the pilot doesn't correct its heading, the plane will fly directly into the storm.

While I believe passive investments are wonderful investments, I believe they are only good during a rising or sideways trend. Otherwise, the likelihood of investment loss is high.

Before moving on to William's story, I want to use David's asset allocation decision as an example to stress a very important point. Some investors and investment professionals alike are unaware of the existence of trends. As such, they attempt to manage risk by allocating money between "risky" investments, like stocks, and "less risky" investments, like bonds. By doing so, they claim they are managing risk by only investing "some" money in the stock market. But here's the rub.

The money they chose to invest in bond investments is not really at risk. It's the money invested in stock investments that is. So, consider David's choice once again. Whether David chooses to invest 25 percent, 50 percent, 75 percent, or more of his money in the stock market, future performance returns are likely to be highly dependent on the trend. Right now, he has chosen to invest 20 percent in the stock market. In other words, without being aware of trends, he is essentially "hoping" the current rising trend continues. Otherwise, he is likely to experience some form of investment loss in the future when the trend changes.

In my opinion, one of David's greatest risks is a continued rising trend. Why? Because if prices rise and he makes more money on his stock investment than what he is making on his CDs, what might greed and fear cause him to do? He may become greedy for more return and fearful of "missing out" on potential gains. This may cause him to move more money out of CDs and into his stock investments at higher and potentially riskier prices. Should that happen and a trend correction takes place thereafter, his later purchases may exacerbate future investment loss.

Now let's visit with William.

William's Story

William started his business out of his garage in the early 1990s. Over the next 18 years, it grew to 24 full-time employees. But when the last economic recession hit, it hit them hard. Their trusted financial professionals initially assured them the economic contraction wouldn't be significant or last long. But by the time the contraction bottomed, they had laid off 60 percent of their employees and burned through 90 percent of their savings.

As the economy began to recover, so did their business. After making a strategic change to their business model, their revenues eventually recovered to where they had been before the downturn. But then William's business partner passed away unexpectedly and he decided it was time to sell. He also feared another recession could wipe him out. He began searching for a buyer and eventually found one. In an interesting twist of fate, the due diligence process took longer than expected, allowing another potential buyer to come to the table with a second offer that was 40 percent higher than the first. William sold the company to the highest bidder, was offered a position on staff, and decided to remain.

William's Decision

Unlike David, William had been investing money outside his business for most of the years leading up to the sale. And since he was already working with an investment professional before the sale, he didn't see a reason to change.

William's financial investments consist primarily of cash equivalents, actively managed stock and bond mutual funds, and some exchange-traded funds (ETFs) as well.

William's Investment Strategy and Outlook

William is using a Buy & Substitute investment strategy. Like David, his future investment performance for most of his investments will be primarily dependent on future trends, unless he or his investment professional decide to make a change.

Allow me to add one or two more details to his story. First, when I asked him how his choice of strategy could help protect him against loss during another change in trend, he assured me he would be fine. After all, his investment professional had told him to make sure he lets her know when he is 12 to 18 months away from retiring so she can move more of his money out of his stock investments and into bond investments. But in light of having heard David's story, do you see the potential problem for William?

To make this as clear as possible, let's assume William's money is allocated 75 percent to stock investments and 25 percent to bond and cash equivalent investments. And one day he calls his investment professional and tells her he will retire the following year. In return, she changes his allocation to be more conservative, possibly by reducing his stock investments to 60 percent and his bond and cash equivalent investments to 40 percent.

While this may help reduce *some* of his potential investment loss from a trend correction, he will still have 60 percent of his investments left to the mercy of the trend! In other words, while he may have safely tucked away some money to use if stock market prices drop significantly, does that suggest he should blindly accept losing 30 percent, 40 percent, or even 50 percent of the remaining value of his stock investments? I certainly hope not.

The second detail I want to point out is the potentially mis-allocated credit William is giving his investment professional. When he was saving money during the years before his business sale, his choice of strategy predominately followed the prevailing stock market trend. When the trend was declining during the past economic contractions, so did the value of his investments. Then when the trend turned back up, so did the value of his investments. He credits his investment professional with his investment gains. But it may only be a coincidence. The gains he is currently experiencing in his stock investments may have more to do with the current rising trend than the specific choices of stock mutual funds.

Remember, a rising tide lifts all boats. When the tide recedes again in the future, what do you think is likely to happen to the value of William's stock investments? I believe he should expect them to decline. Depending on the size of the decline, it could have a lasting negative impact on his financial wealth.

Now I'd like you to meet Martin.

Martin's Story

Martin purchased his company from his father in the mid-1980s, while it was generating $1 million in annual revenue. His father wanted to retire but could not find a buyer. Since Martin didn't have the cash, or ability to get a loan to buy it from him, his father owner-financed the sale over 10 years.

Over the next 33 years, Martin grew the company to a staff of 30 full-time employees. The company generated annual revenues close to $20 million. But the trade-off to this success was a diminishing quality of life. And in 2018, when he was diagnosed with some health-related issues, he sold the business.

Martin's Decision

Martin had invested outside the business during his working years and in the process acquired many rental real estate properties, all of which he continues to own today. He also made investments in the stock market, accumulating a significant number of shares in one stock. And like William, Martin had worked with an investment professional before the sale and decided to maintain that professional relationship.

Martin's Investment Strategy and Outlook

Unlike William, Martin decided to use a Buy & Sell strategy after his sale for the portion of his wealth invested in the stock market. You may recall that like Buy & Substitute, this also is an active management strategy. But it differs in that it may not remain fully invested all the time. Based on its name (Buy & Sell), some type of sell process tends to accompany this strategy to help limit investment loss, if possible.

If Martin's Buy & Sell strategy successfully manages downside risk over the long term, it offers him an opportunity that is not available with the other two strategies. Martin may decide to allocate a larger portion of his money to stock investments. Compared to potentially lower returns on some bond or cash equivalent investments, this could help him continue to grow his wealth, at least when trends are rising. Of course, there are no guarantees he will be successful.

Suppose Martin decided to invest 75 percent of his sale proceeds to stock investments. Referring once again to the speed limit example in Chapter 6, it means Martin *may* have the entire 75 percent invested in stock investments sometimes, but not necessarily always. Even though he has allocated 75 percent to stocks, there may be times when his investment professional may choose to leave a portion in cash-equivalent investments, or possibly inverse ETFs, if warranted.

KEY TAKEAWAYS

If you can relate to David, William, or Martin, you likely understand how it can take many years, if not decades, to accumulate financial wealth. And after reading Chapter 6, you can now see from a historical perspective how a significant portion of your financial wealth could be lost in a relatively short period of time. At the time I met David, William, and Martin, none of them were aware of financial market trends and the potential loss they might experience when the next channel or trend correction comes to pass. If they were, some of them may be inclined to reconsider their choice of investment strategy. George Santayana said, "Those who cannot remember the past are condemned to repeat it."

As for Mallory? It wasn't long after suffering her losses that she began to make changes to her "long-term" investment plan. She sold some investments shortly after the lows to make new investments in other investment categories, like real estate, hoping to make back some of her losses. Had she initially used an investment strategy that could have helped limit some of her losses, I believe she may not have been inclined to take that action.

CHAPTER 9

Costly Oversights

Beware of little expenses.
A small leak will sink a great ship.

—Benjamin Franklin

In the previous chapter, I shared the stories of
three people who became financially wealthy and how they
decided to invest their wealth. In this chapter, I will share
the story of a fourth individual, whom I will call Earl. His
story differs from the others because he has not yet made his
decision and it provides an opportunity to introduce some
additional concepts you may find beneficial.

Earl's Story

Earl owned and operated a successful specialty sign business
in the early 2000s that employed 12 full-time employees at
its peak. But when the economy turned down with the recession of 2007, his business suffered, and like William, he
was forced to lay off two-thirds of his staff. Fortunately, his
business survived and eventually improved along with the
overall economy. It took several years for his business revenues

to recover to pre-recession levels, but even with his business on the mend, he suffered from fear and anxiety over "the next" economic downturn. The worry and stress took a toll on his health, leading him to sell his operating business in 2015.

The deal included terms for the buyer to exercise an option to purchase his commercial building within five years at a favorable market price. Four and a half years later, the buyer exercised the option and bought the building. Earl paid income taxes on the sale and deposited a seven-figure check into his brokerage account. Having already invested the money from the sale of his operating business, he now faced the decision of how to invest the sale proceeds from the building.

Earl had been working with the same investment professional for 18 years, and when he sat down to discuss his investment options, he was presented with the recommendations in Table 9A.

Earl had never doubted his investment professional before, but he discovered that the professional's recommendation overlooked several small, yet potentially significant, expenses that could be problematic. These expenses include *lost fee discounts*, *unearned tax liabilities*, and continued *interest expenses*.

Table 9A

INVESTMENT:	SYMBOL:	ALLOCATION:
BUCKET 1: "Stable value investments"		
Guggenheim Limited Duration Fund	GILHX	3.3%
Guggenheim High Yield Fund	SHYIX	3.3%
Nuveen Managed Muni Portfolio	N/A	8.9%
Vanguard Wellesley Income	VWINX	4.4%
BUCKET 2: "Alternative income sources"		
Nationwide Immediate Income Annuity	N/A	11.1%
Blackstone real estate investment	N/A	4.4%
Structured product	N/A	4.4%
BUCKET 3: "Growth-biased investments"		
Alger Small Cap Focus	AOFYX	2.2%
American Funds Capital Income Builder	CAIFX	4.4%
Boston Partners All Cap Value	BPAIX	6.7%
Chiron Capital Allocation	CCAPX	6.7%
First Eagle Global	SGIIX	4.4%
Guggenheim Total Return Bond	GIBIX	4.4%
JP Morgan Income Builder	JNBSX	4.4%
Western Asset Core Plus Bond	WACPX	4.4%
CIO High Quality Dividend Yield Portfolio	N/A	22.2%

FEE DISCOUNTS

The Book of Luke 10:7 says, "The labourer is worthy of their hire." In the investment industry, there are several different ways your investment professional may be compensated for their services. One way is through fees paid through *financial products*, and a second way is through fees paid as an annual percent on the value of your investment account, called an *asset management fee.* The difference between the two could be significant over time.

Financial Product Fees

When you compensate your investment professional through financial products, the fee is set by prospectus. In other words, the company offering the financial product maintains absolute control over the amount charged and only they can change it. Your investment professional has no say in the matter whatsoever. While this may not be very important with smaller account balances, it can be very important with larger account balances.

For instance, "Stephen" was a licensed investment professional who worked for Legg Mason in the late 1990s. He exclusively recommended the proprietary Legg Mason mutual funds to his clients as an investment solution, and while there was no sales charge or commission for investors to buy into or sell out of the funds, they did have an internal 1 percent annual fee that compensated Legg Mason and Stephen.

Stephen's largest client at that time had investment accounts worth over $6 million in total, all invested in Legg Mason mutual funds. In other words, with a fixed 1 percent fee, his client was paying $60,000 per year in fees for his services. Is that reasonable? Only the client can be the judge. But to stress my point further, what if their accounts were worth $12 million? With a fixed fee of 1 percent, his client would have been paying $120,000 in annual fees. Since at the time the fees were not transparent in terms of actual dollars paid, it could be easy to dodge the amount of *dollars* paid by referring to them in terms of a *percent*.

Asset Management Fees

Alternatively, when your investment professional is compensated through asset management fees, not only is the fee completely transparent but in some cases it may be negotiable. It is transparent because the fee can be deducted directly from your account on a monthly or quarterly basis as a separate line item so you know exactly how much you are paying for services provided. It may be negotiable because the firm the investment professional represents, or the investment professional themselves, sets the fee—not the financial product company.

What you should know is there are two types of asset management fees, *flat* and *tiered*. A *flat* asset management fee would be similar to the example above, where your investment professional is compensated at a flat annual rate, regardless of the value of your investment account. For instance, whether your investment account value is $500,000 or $5 million, the fee remains flat. There is no adjustment unless you are able to negotiate a different rate.

For instance, had Stephen used a *flat* one percent asset management fee when working with the client above, they still would have paid $60,000 per year, but at least the fee would have been transparent. And unlike the financial product fee, the asset management fee may have been tax-deductible at that time. In other words, if the fee was paid using after-tax dollars, part of the fee may have been eligible for a tax-deduction, essentially lowering the effective fee further.

A second option is a *tiered* asset management fee, and unlike a flat fee, this structure may effectively reduce your fees should your investment accounts increase in value over time. For instance, suppose Stephen used a tiered fee structure with this client. It might have looked something like this:

On the *first* $1 million	1.00 percent
On the *next* $2 million	0.80 percent
On the *next* $2 million	0.60 percent
Over $5 million	0.50 percent

In other words, on the first $1 million, Stephen's client would have paid $10,000 per year. On the next $2 million, they would have paid $16,000 per year. On the next $2 million, they would have paid $12,000 per year. And on the last $1 million, they would have paid $5,000 per year. So, instead of paying $60,000 in annual fees through the financial product or under a flat fee, Stephen's clients' effective annual fee could have been $43,000 per year, or 0.72 percent annually under a tiered fee schedule.

So how does all this apply to Earl? Earl's investment professional quoted him a flat asset management fee of 1 percent on the sale proceeds from his commercial building. But here's the rub. The investments that Earl previously purchased with the sale proceeds from his operating business back in 2015 are invested in financial products that compensate his professional through the financial products. This raises two potential problems.

First, the fees paid through the financial products are not transparent, while those from the asset management fees are. This may lead Earl to mistakenly believe the total fees he is paying are lower than they are.

Second, the financial products[15] Earl already owns are not eligible to be counted under the asset management fee schedule. Do you see the problem? The more money Earl has invested under an asset management fee (especially a tiered asset management fee), the lower his total annual fees could be compared to what they may be with the current investment recommendations.

If Earl consents to his investment professional's recommendation and continues to use two different types of compensation arrangements, he will forego potential fee discounts that could save him thousands of dollars each year while in receipt of the same services.

UNEARNED TAX LIABILITIES

The sale of Earl's commercial property in 2019 resulted in a taxable gain. And while he didn't relish paying taxes on the sale, the value of the property did appreciate during the years he owned it. While he may find paying taxes on his own personal gains acceptable, he may find paying taxes on someone else's gains completely unacceptable. But with his investment professional's recommendation in Table 9A, Earl may do just that.

The stock market has been rising for the past several years, and what Earl may not realize is some of the recommended stock mutual funds contain unrealized taxable gains. While purchasing these funds in a tax-deferred account (a 401(k) or an IRA) would not pose a problem, purchasing these funds with after-tax money may. Let me explain why.

If Earl purchases an actively managed mutual fund, he won't just buy the underlying securities on that day's closing prices, he *will also buy their unrealized taxable gains*. If one of the stock mutual funds purchased shares of ABC stock five years ago at $15 per share and shares of ABC are valued today at $30 per share, when Earl purchases the mutual fund, not only will he purchase ABC stock at today's price of $30 per share, he will also buy into the unrealized taxable gain of $15.

Suppose shortly after Earl purchases the mutual fund, ABC stock is sold for $35 a share. Earl will only have to pay taxes on the difference between $30 and $35 dollars, right? Wrong! He will have to pay his proportionate share of any taxes owed on the entire gain, even though he never benefitted from the share price appreciation from $15 to $30.

During calendar year 2019, several of the stock mutual funds listed in Table 9A had appreciated share prices on securities that had been purchased years earlier. In other words, if any stocks with unrealized gains were sold shortly after Earl purchases the mutual fund, he may be liable for his proportion of the taxes owed on those gains, even though he didn't receive much of a financial benefit.

Talk about adding insult to injury! Earl just paid thousands of dollars in taxes on the sale of his commercial property, and the recommendations he received from his trusted investment professional could cost him hundreds or thousands of dollars more in unnecessary taxes.

Does this mean Earl should not invest in any actively managed stock mutual funds? Absolutely not. But to avoid potential tax bombs, Earl has to identify the potential unrealized capital gains tax exposure before purchasing them, especially when using after-tax money for the purchase. There are two ways he can do this.

First, a quick but unofficial way is to visit Morningstar.com. (At the time of this book's writing, this service is available and free.)

- On the site, he would enter the symbol of the mutual fund in the upper left-hand corner where it says **Search Quotes and Site**.

- Next, he would click on the name of the fund, which should take him to a fund details page. Beneath the mutual fund name is a tab labeled **Price.** He would click it.

- Next, he would scroll down the page to where it says **Potential Capital Gains Exposure**. This provides the approximate percent of the current share price that is potentially taxable. The lower this number, the better, when you are using after-tax money to purchase the mutual fund.

Alternatively, if he wants an absolute number, he could call each mutual fund company directly and ask their customer service center for the most up-to-date tax information on the fund.

If the potential capital gains taxes are high (10 percent or more), he may want to consider other investment options, at least until the potential unrealized taxable gains become less. This could happen from either future stock sales or a price correction in the stock market.

INTEREST EXPENSES

Interest expenses, especially those that are nondeductible, can also become significant expenses over time. Before he sold his commercial building, Earl used his investment account as collateral for a pledged account to borrow money to buy his new house. He chose this method as a faster and more convenient option than applying for a conventional mortgage. His investment firm charged him interest on the loan, at a variable rate tied to the London Inter-bank Offered Rate (LIBOR) with no amortization or payoff schedule. LIBOR is a benchmark interest rate at which major global banks lend to one another in the international interbank market for short-term loans.

Strangely, when his broker provided his recommendation in Table 9A, he did not include any provision to pay off this debt. The monthly interest expense was costing Earl over $2,500 per month, or $30,000 per year, at the time.

Once Earl became aware of these issues, he was concerned. After working with his investment professional for 18 years, he began to wonder if this was still the right investment professional for him. But Earl wants to give him the benefit of the doubt. He wants to know how his investment professional would recommend going about the investment of his wealth in the stock market. That will be the topic of discussion for the next chapter.

KEY TAKEAWAY

It is common for investors to trust the recommendations of their investment professionals. After all, that is why they initially hired them. But it is important you are aware of some of these small details so you can ask about them before they become problems later, helping you to avoid unnecessary expenses.

As for Mallory, she bought into actively managed stock mutual funds five years after the stock market low in early 2003. While she was unable to locate her statements after so many years, it is very possible she may have bought into some unrealized capital gains. And when the stock market began declining in earnest, it's possible that forced sales from shareholder redemptions could have resulted in her having to pay some taxes on other investors' previous gains.

CHAPTER 10

Timing Is Everything

The entrance strategy is actually
more important than the exit strategy.

–EDWARD LAMPERT

EARL FACES A DILEMMA. FIRST, AFTER DISCOVERING several significant oversights by his financial professional identified in the previous chapter, his trust is a little shaken. But they have worked together for a long time and Earl doesn't want to end their professional relationship for that reason alone. He has decided to pay a little more attention to the remaining details of his investment professional's recommendation. Specifically, Earl wants to look at how his advisor recommends buying into the stock market.

Earl's most significant concern is losing money. It took him his working lifetime to accumulate his wealth, and now he is faced with making investment decisions of which he knows little. Since he first sold his operating business, the stock market has gone up and has reached new "all-time highs." This can be seen in Chart 10A of the S&P 500 Index, that spans calendar year 2015 through the first half of 2019.

CHART 10A

Chart courtesy of Stockcharts.com

Even though he will only be investing a portion of his financial wealth in the stock market, the dollar amount is seven digits and he wants to know how his investment professional recommends he buy in. Earl's investment professional explains there are four predominate ways for him to buy into his stock mutual funds: *Dollar-cost-averaging, selective purchases,* a *lump-sum purchase,* and a *deferred purchase.* Before explaining these options, consider the following story.

THE POT ROAST STORY

A young girl noticed her mom cutting off the ends of a pot roast before putting it in the oven. She had seen her do this many times before but had never asked why. This time she asked, and her mother replied, "I don't know. *My mother always did it that way* and I learned from her. Why don't you ask your grandmother?"

The young girl called her grandmother and asked why she cut the ends off the pot roast before cooking it. Her grandmother replied, "I don't know. That's just the way my mother always did it."

Undeterred, the young girl called her great-grandmother and asked the same question. Why did you cut the ends off the pot roast before cooking it? Great-grandmother replied, "Well, when I was first married, we had a very small oven and the pot roast didn't fit unless I cut the ends off first."

The story above helps illustrate an important point—asking the question, "Why?" Some investors, and investment professionals alike, make investment decisions every day according to the way it has always been done before. In this story, two generations are doing things the way the previous generation did them without asking why. When the little girl finally asked the question, she discovered a reference point—the oven. As the following four buy-in options are explained, is there a common reference point Earl could use to help with his decision?

DOLLAR-COST-AVERAGING (DCA)

DCA is a common strategy used by investors when buying financial investments, especially investments in the stock market. It consists of making a series of equal purchases spread out over a predetermined period. In this option, the portion of Earl's money that will be invested in each stock mutual fund would be divided into equal-sized amounts and purchases will take place over a few months, if not longer. For instance, if $300,000 was going to be invested in one specific stock mutual fund, Earl might consider the following options:

- $100,000 each month, spread out over 3 months

- $50,000 each month, spread out over 6 months

- $25,000 each month, spread out over 12 months

But if Earl's purchases are completed quickly and the stock market "tops out" thereafter, he would be fully invested and could suffer loss, depending on his choice of strategy. Alternatively, if his purchases are spread out over a longer period and the stock market continues to rise, he would be paying more with each purchase, increasing his future potential risk for loss if the stock market "tops out" after he becomes fully invested.

SELECTIVE PURCHASES

With this option, Earl's purchases would be completed in several transactions but these transactions do not take place over a predetermined timeline. This option may prove beneficial when buying stock investments that tend to experience higher than average price volatility or when a rising stock market trend may be in the process of changing to a sideways or declining trend. It is called selective because in contrast to a dollar-cost-averaging strategy where equal purchases take place over a set schedule with selective purchases, each investment is evaluated individually.

LUMP-SUM PURCHASE

With this option, Earl's purchases would be completed in a single transaction. While people typically use it to buy investments that experience little-to-no price volatility, like an immediate annuity, this option may prove beneficial for use with stock investments under certain circumstances.

For instance, if the timing of Earl's sale coincided with a declining stock market trend that had lasted for one, two, or even three years, buying all his stock investments in a lump sum might prove beneficial over the long term. While such trends do not come along often, they may provide an opportunity to buy in at prices that could be 20 to 50 percent lower from the top price. Several historical periods where this option could have proven beneficial, at least in hindsight, include calendar years 1969 to 1970, 1973 to 1974, 1981 to 1982, the 1987 "crash," 2000 to 2002, and 2008 into early 2009.

DEFERRED PURCHASE

With this option, Earl may make the conscious choice to refrain from investing his money for an indefinite period. You might be more inclined to choose this option if the timing of his sale coincided with an ongoing declining trend, like 1940 to1941, 1973 to 1974, and 2000 to 2002, illustrated in Chapter 1. During these relatively short historical windows he might be better off holding cash and collecting some interest while waiting for the declining trend to come to an end before buying in. Since Earl is in possession of a relatively large amount of cash, he might want to keep in mind two old adages: "Cash is king" and "Buy low, sell high."

With that said, you may think I am referring to market timing, but that is not how I intend it. I believe true "market timing" pertains to short-term trading decisions over the course of hours, days, or even weeks. But when referring to a deferred purchase for the purposes of this chapter, it is in the context of a declining trend. Declining trends referenced within this book historically last from one to three years.

Like the pot roast story above where the little girl discovered the oven was the reference point, I believe the prevailing trend is a potential reference point Earl could use to help him make his buy-in decision.

Since the purpose of this book is to help illustrate some of the potential benefits of following trends, Chart 10A has been updated in Chart 10B to reflect what I believe is the primary trend at the time Earl was considering his decision.

CHART 10B

Chart courtesy of Stockcharts.com

If this rising trend is identified correctly, Earl could use it to help him make his buy-in decision through a process of elimination. For instance, based upon the past several years of history, the stock market has been enjoying a rising primary trend. Unless this continues forever (which is not likely), the current rising trend could change and turn into a declining trend. Since Earl is very concerned about financial loss, he would likely eliminate the lump sum option.

Next, since the investments he intends to purchase consist of stock mutual funds and his purchases only take effect at the end-of-day closing prices, it could be difficult to make selective purchases. So Earl might be inclined to eliminate that as an option as well.

This leaves him with two remaining options—DCA or a deferred purchase. If Earl viewed his remaining two options from the perspective of this potential rising trend, he might conclude his best option at that immediate moment would be a deferred purchase. While the trend can't predict what the stock market will do next, Earl may prefer to defer his buy-in at that moment but begin using the DCA option *if* price declines to the bottom of the trend. After all, as you learned in Chapter 6, trend corrections are historically more likely to happen when price declines below the bottom trend line. So deferring for now and targeting that area for the *first* DCA purchase might be something he is more comfortable with. If price continues to drop after that purchase, he could defer additional purchases. If they continue to rise, Earl may have a greater amount of confidence that he is buying in at what he believes to be the "bottom" of the rising trend.

From personal experience during my career, I have found DCA is the more commonly used option and the deferred option the least common. And while DCA can be used successfully most of the time, without the use of a reference point, two specific circumstances can arise when it is outright detrimental.

The first would arise if Earl finishes his last purchase shortly before or just after a rising trend changes into a declining trend. The second would arise if both Earl and his investment professional were not aware of stock market trends at all. What if they began purchasing and continued purchasing when the stock market was already in a declining trend? Each purchase could result in further financial loss. While it may be convenient to believe that the DCA option may afford the "accumulation" of stock shares at many different prices, providing for a good "average" purchase price when the buy-in is finished, is that what Earl really wants with his money? No.

KEY TAKEAWAYS

When faced with a purchase decision in the stock market, or any financial market for that matter, using a reference point can be helpful. This can be especially true if the amount of money or wealth is relatively large. If you can correctly identify the primary trend, it can help eliminate options that might result in financial loss in the absence of using the trend. While no strategy can guarantee success, using the trend may help you eliminate several of the less desirable options, at least at that moment in time.

And Mallory? Her investment professional recommended using the DCA strategy to invest her money over three months. And, in my opinion, there was nothing wrong with that recommendation. The stock market was experiencing a rising trend at that time, and it would be logical to make purchases over a shorter, rather than longer, period under such circumstances. Unfortunately, the trend changed shortly thereafter, and since Mallory was using an investment strategy that could not, and would not, adapt to that change, she suffered loss.[16]

CHAPTER 11

Hiring a Professional Is as Easy as 1-2-3

If you think it's expensive to hire a professional,
wait until you hire an amateur.

–RED ADAIR

AFTER LEARNING OF EARL'S EXPERIENCES IN THE preceding two chapters, you might not be surprised to hear that he is contemplating changing his investment professional. Supposing he does, will he ultimately find who he is looking for? Let me tell you a story to help clarify what I mean.

I became a licensed investment professional in late 1997, and in one of my training classes I was told a story I have always remembered. Around that time there was a no-load, or "do-it-yourself" asset management company, like Vanguard, who offered their financial products directly to individual investors: clients could buy their financial products without having to purchase them through an investment professional. And over time, this company noticed a concerning trend—they were losing customers to full-service investment firms. As they researched this ongoing exodus further, they discovered that on average, when the combined balances of some customers' accounts exceeded a certain dollar amount, their concern of losing money from a bad investment decision caused them to seek help from a licensed investment professional. Apparently, when their account values equaled or exceeded $333,000, their perspective of a professional's fee changed and it became a value rather than an expense. This caused some customers to transfer their investment accounts to full-service investment professionals.

Now I want you to consider this question: Do you think the customers found what they were looking for? Would any investment professional suffice? Or were they looking for someone specific? How might the customers research, identify, and find an individual or group that would work for them?

Earl now finds himself in a similar situation. And if, like him, you are considering replacing your existing investment professional, or possibly hiring your first, I propose three steps that may help you with your search. The first step is to identify and choose your preferred investment *philosophy*. The second step is to identify and choose your preferred investment *strategy*. And the third and final step is to interview and choose your preferred *investment professional(s)*.

STEP 1: CHOOSE YOUR INVESTMENT PHILOSOPHY

First off, you need to understand that your investment philosophy and strategy are not the same. Your investment philosophy stems from what you *believe,* while your investment strategy is *how* you intend to accomplish your belief.

This was the topic of a *Forbes* article written by Rick Ferri in June 2014 titled, "Philosophy Differs from Strategy." Like Rick, I believe it is important to choose your investment philosophy and adhere to it firmly over time because, as Rick writes in the article, "Philosophy acts as the glue that holds everything together."

As a quick reminder, this book's philosophy is based on a form of technical investing called trend following. Technical investing believes past market data can be used to help identify future patterns on which to base purchase and sell decisions.

Once you identify and decide on your preferred investment philosophy, the next step is to choose your investment strategy.

STEP 2: CHOOSE YOUR INVESTMENT STRATEGY

Back in Chapter 4, I introduced three types of investment strategy—Buy & Hold, Buy & Substitute, and Buy & Sell. While these three are not all-inclusive, I believe they constitute the more common options.

One of the three may be more suitable for you than the others, depending on a number of factors. These factors may include, but are not limited to, current financial market trends, the amount of money you have to invest, how long your invest-ment time horizon is, your phase of life, the proportion of your wealth held in after-tax versus pre-tax accounts, and your individual tax situation.

For instance, if you are younger and are still accumulating your wealth through your company's 401(k) plan, a Buy & Hold or Buy & Substitute strategy (or both!) may be your best option. I say this because most 401(k) plans offer stock mutual funds and, in my opinion, are not the type of investment that is conducive to strategies that may make strategic changes over time, like Buy & Sell.

Alternatively, if you are older and have accumulated your wealth through one of the examples referenced in Chapter 8, then Buy & Sell may be one of your better options (depending on the primary trend at that point in your life).

Once you identify and decide on your preferred investment strategy, the next step is to identify your preferred investment professional(s).

STEP 3: CHOOSE YOUR INVESTMENT PROFESSIONAL(S)

According to the Financial Industry Regulatory Authority (FINRA) website[17], there were almost 630,000 licensed investment professionals ("Registered Representatives") available for hire in 2018. A Registered Representative (RR), or broker, is a person who works for a brokerage company and *purchases* financial products like stocks, bonds, and mutual funds on behalf of their clients. Adding Investment Advisor

Representatives (IARs) to this group increases the number by almost 13,000[18] more. An IAR is a person who is registered with a Registered Investment Advisor (RIA) firm and whose primary responsibility is to provide investment-related *advice* to their clients.

With so many licensed investment professionals available for hire, how can you narrow them down to focus only on those individuals who are your *preferred* candidates? Having completed the first two steps above, you have already eliminated those who offer services that do not meet your initial criteria. In order to reduce this number further, you might differentiate them using the four Cs—*category, capacity, compensation,* and potential *conflicts of interest.* The answers to the four Cs may lead you to one of the more important factors—*incentive.*

THE EMPLOYEE

The first *category* is the employee. This person may be referred to as a generalist, or someone who has variable or unspecialized knowledge. An employee works in a *capacity* that tends to be captive rather than independent. At first, the idea of working with someone who is an employee of a bank or a similar financial institution may seem appealing since their *compensation* may not be tied to the sales of financial products that pay commissions or advisory fees. As such, you may believe this eliminates any potential *conflicts of interest.* But that may not necessarily be true.

For instance, consider the salaried employee working as a client-service representative at Vanguard. They are prohibited from providing individual investment advice to customers. Instead, they predominately provide financial product information, leaving it up to the customer to make their own investment decision.

Or how about someone who works as an employee for a bank or similar financial institution? I once knew a woman who was hired as a salaried employee for a national bank. But her quarterly bonuses were based on her sales of specific financial products that generated commissions for the bank. Sometimes it was from the sale of specific mutual funds, while at other times it was from the sale of certain variable annuities. In such cases, a significant conflict of interest can arise because her incentive was for personal financial gain, not necessarily what was best for the customer.

"Sam" and his family have retirement accounts invested with The Vanguard Group. And one of the selling points of the representative they work with is that the representatives are salaried so there are allegedly no conflicts of interest. After all, Vanguard does not charge any front-end or back-end sales charges on the purchase or sale of their mutual funds. And while Sam and his family like this concept in theory, they have since come to realize that their representative will still be compensated regardless of their financial results.

If you think back to Chapter 1, you may remember that the investment results of the financial products offered by

Vanguard are directly tied to the trend of the financial markets. So while the current rising trend is resulting in positive investment returns on some of their stock mutual funds, what is likely to happen to Sam's investments during the next trend correction? Will the Vanguard employee tell them to sell their investments? No, because Vanguard's philosophy and strategy is to remain fully invested. So in such a circumstance, the employee will receive their compensation while the customers' investment accounts lose value.

THE BROKER

The second category is the broker. Like the employee, in some cases this individual may also be referred to as a generalist. "Peter" has been a business attorney for over 30 years and shared his personal observations from meeting many brokers throughout the course of his career. He compares some of them to a vending machine.

For instance, if an investor wants to save money for their children's college expenses, the broker will push button "E1" on the vending machine and out pops a recommendation for a 529 college savings plan. If a business owner wants to save money for retirement outside their business, the broker will push button "R2" on the vending machine and out pops a recommendation for a SIMPLE IRA retirement plan. And if someone needs life insurance, the licensed broker will push button "I4" on the vending machine and out pops a recommendation for a whole life or term insurance policy.

While there is nothing necessarily wrong with any of these recommendations, I believe Peter was trying to make the point that the minute there was an opportunity to make a "sale," the broker jumped on it. Since some brokers hold multiple licenses, they may offer a broad range of financial products and investment solutions to be a "one-stop shop" for their clients' financial service needs. In such circumstances, they may be a jack of all trades and a master of none.

Depending on the firm that holds the broker's investment license, the broker may work in a capacity that is either captive or independent. For instance, consider a broker who represents a firm like Edward Jones. According to the article titled "Edward Jones Agrees to Settle Host of Charges"[19] that appeared in *The Wall Street Journal* on December 21, 2004,

> "Edward D. Jones & Co. agreed to pay $75 million to settle regulatory charges that it steered investors to seven 'preferred' mutual-fund groups, without telling the investors that the firm received hundreds of millions of dollars in compensation from those funds."

So how could you determine whether a broker's recommendation is due to their captive status with the firm, as opposed to an independent status with you as their client? A captive broker may be more compelled to recommend specific financial products promoted by their firm, while an independent broker may be able to avoid such situations completely.

The broker is compensated through commissions paid on the sale of financial products, as well as fees based on your account's value. And while commissions on product sales are not necessarily bad, they do create the potential for conflicts of interest, especially when the commissions are paid through the financial product and are not transparent. This tends to be more prevalent with the sale of some variable annuities, private investments, and certain life insurance products. Whenever commissions are involved, it can be difficult to identify the broker's true incentive. Is it the right financial product to solve your financial need? Or will it just generate commissions for the broker and their firm? It is not always easy to differentiate between the two.

THE PLANNER

The third category is the planner. This person usually specializes in a specific area, such as planning for retirement or planning for your children's future college expenses. The planner tends to work in an independent capacity and earns their compensation through a contractual hourly rate, flat rate, or monthly recurring rate. Their fee is 100 percent transparent and the fee-only planner does not receive any compensation through financial product sales. As a result, conflicts of interest tend to be nonexistent.

An independent planner offers help with building a financial plan. Their process may include advice on how to plan for your retirement, manage your estate, reduce your income taxes, or which financial investments to use depending on your specific financial goals. Their incentive is to offer advice that solves your need.

"Oliver" found himself in a dilemma. He had one daughter in college, a second getting ready to begin her freshman year, and a third in her later years of high school. He was in need of very specialized advice on different financing options to help pay college tuition bills. After interviewing a few people, he hired the planner who charged an hourly fee and specialized in college financing options rather than the other alleged "planners" who give advice but made their money through the sale of financial products. Oliver wanted to work with someone he felt was providing independent, unbiased advice, and he was happy to compensate them for their expertise. What he didn't want was someone who provided advice but whose compensation came through his purchase of a financial product.

THE FEE-ONLY ADVISOR

The fourth category is the fee-only advisor. Like the planner, this person may also be a specialist. The fee-only advisor tends to work for a Registered Investment Advisor (RIA) in an independent capacity. They earn their compensation through the fees charged for their services, either as a percent of the value of your account, or through a contractual agreement. Their compensation is 100 percent transparent, and since this professional is not compensated through commissions from financial product sales, conflicts of interest tend to be non-existent.

The fee-only advisor's financial incentive is aligned with you for a very distinct reason—they only receive compensation while you retain their services. If they don't receive any sales commissions when they make your initial purchases, there are no back-end sales charges that could prevent you from selling your securities at a cost to you thereafter, and if the securities purchased on your behalf can be freely transferred to another professional with your signature, then I believe that establishes a proper incentive.

Some fee-only advisors offer a unique strategy or process in exchange for their compensation. For instance, one may offer an investment strategy that only invests in a limited number of stocks held within the S&P 500 Index, predominately those companies that meet the definition of "large cap." Another may only invest in the stocks of small companies that meet a definition of "small cap."

In many cases, the financial investments they use tend to be those you could purchase directly yourself. So, if your results don't meet your standards over a reasonable period, such as five or 10 years, it is relatively easy to change advisors. All you need do is to repeat the process of seeking out another professional who possesses the same philosophy and offers a similar strategy. Then you may be able to transfer your investments in-kind for them to manage. This can be very beneficial compared to situations where you may have to pay a sales charge to exit one of your investments, or if you have paid a sales commission up front to purchase an investment in the first place.

A WORD OF CAUTION

Throughout my career, I have observed some investors try to "diversify" their investment professionals by working with more than one. Personally, I do not believe this is a good idea for two reasons. First, too much information can cause confusion. And second, depending on the category of investment professional you hire, *you* may create conflicts of interest.

For instance, since some brokers offer the same financial products and services, if you decide to hire two or more, you might experience a situation where they begin competing against each other to try and earn more of your business. They may take risks with your money to try to earn higher returns to justify why you should transfer all your wealth to them. But is this really what you want? Your trusted investment professionals competing against each other rather than making decisions that are in your best interest?

I believe the preferred way to hire two or more investment professionals is when they complement rather than compete against, each other. For instance, under the fee-only advisor discussion above, I mentioned one fee-only advisor whose strategy only invests in stocks that are included in the S&P 500 Index, typically those that are larger-sized companies. The other fee-only advisor's strategy only invests in smaller-sized companies. Since they each focus on different segments of the stock market, I believe they are more likely to complement each other and manage their individual strategy for your long-term benefit.

KEY TAKEAWAYS

Of the four categories of licensed investment professionals identified in this lesson, is there a wrong choice? Yes: when you hire someone who does not share your philosophy and preferred strategy. I believe it is your responsibility and in your best interest to educate yourself on how these professionals differ so you can spend your time seeking out only those individuals who are best suited to offer what you are looking for. In my personal experience, people usually follow the three steps I've outlined above in reverse order, or not at all.

As for Mallory, her first investment professional happened to be a broker, and when Mallory hired her, Mallory defaulted to her broker's philosophy and strategy. Since this first experience, she has changed investment professionals twice more beginning the process all over again each time. Had she followed a different due diligence process and if she knew more of what to ask, she could have had a different outcome and might still be working with her original professional today.

CHAPTER 12

Protective Pillars

It is better to look ahead and prepare
than to look back and regret.

–Jackie Joyner-Kersee

I hope you have learned a lot over the past few chapters through Earl's story. Earl himself has been discovering many new concepts he had been unaware of previously. Based on the three steps outlined in Chapter 11, he has identified his preferred investment philosophy, identified his preferred investment strategy, and narrowed the field of preferred investment professionals to fewer than a handful. So, who will he choose to hire?

As he was ready to make his decision, he came across an article on the web that caused some hesitation. Reuters published an article on January 24, 2020 titled, "Owners of solar company that caused loss for Buffett plead guilty over Ponzi scheme."[20] According to the story, Warren Buffett's Berkshire Hathaway had to take a $377 million charge to earnings last year due to losses associated with this scheme. This story triggered Earl's memory about another story that made headline news back in 2008. That story was about an investment firm that was also running a Ponzi scheme where investors in the scheme eventually lost billions, not millions.

The mastermind was Bernie Madoff, and many wealthy investors flocked to his firm because his performance results appeared to defy logic, earning consistent returns with what appeared to be little to no risk. And as client account values increased, human nature took over and more investors poured in, either from greed for gain, fear of missing out, or both. But it eventually came to light that Madoff's firm was creating fraudulent financial statements. The alleged "gains" were nothing more than an illusion.

Before the scheme was discovered, Madoff's clients had complete trust in him. And why wouldn't they? He had a stellar reputation and plenty of noteworthy accomplishments. For instance, he was an upstanding individual in the investment community. He was the head of the firm that helped launch the Nasdaq stock market. He sat on the board of the National Association of Securities Dealers. He had even provided advice to the Securities and Exchange Commission—the very government agency tasked with protecting investors from the crimes he committed. (Sadly, they stood by idly as Madoff "made-off" with his client's fortunes.)

While schemes the scale of Madoff's don't happen often, these two news stories teach an important lesson: no matter who you are or how much money you have, anyone can fall victim to such schemes. Financial loss occurs first, then regret follows thereafter. Grant B. Gelberg writes in *Regret Theory: Explanation, Evaluation and Implications for the Law*:

> "We are all familiar with the would've, could've, and should've beens of life. Whether manifested in the pang of a poor decision or the feeling of an opportunity lost, regret is one of the most profound human emotions. The power of regret has attracted researchers who have studied its impact on decision-making under risk or uncertainty.[21] These studies have spawned regret theory…
>
> "Regret theory asserts two simple assumptions. First, once a decision is made people evaluate the outcome and feel regret if an alternative outcome would have led to a better result. Alternatively, a person rejoices if a different outcome would have made him worse off.[22] Second, regret theory states that people will anticipate these ex post feelings and shift their preferences ex ante."

In other words, after experiencing regret, when faced with a similar decision in the future, your past experiences can create a negative feedback loop where you *anticipate* future regret and account for it in your decision. Consider Mallory's story once again. After losing 42 percent of her investment value in the first 18 months of her long-term investment plan, she suffered tremendous regret. She regretted the trust she placed in her chosen financial institution. She regretted hiring her broker. And she especially regretted her cavalier attitude toward her wealth and investments. The outcome from all this led to Mallory losing confidence in herself and her decisions.

This raises an important question: Is there anything that Mallory, Earl, or you can do to help limit the odds of experiencing regret? I believe there are five foundational pillars that can help prevent regret and protect your confidence.

Pillar #1: People, not paper

When you are evaluating potential candidates to hire as your investment professional, are you influenced by well-branded and familiar company names? Firms like Merrill Lynch, Edward Jones, Charles Schwab, and Vanguard are well-known and well-established and spend a lot of money on advertising to make their brands familiar and memorable. But without the people who work there, a brand is just a fancy imprint on a piece of paper. Merrill Lynch is never going to pick up the telephone and call you but Sally Smith who represents Merrill Lynch may. Build a connection with the person on the other line and develop a trusting relationship with them, not the piece of paper.

"Larry" had been accumulating gold and silver coins for several years, and when gold and silver prices began to rise, he became concerned about theft. So he got a quote from his insurance company, the same one that insured his house and car, to find out what it would cost to insure his collection. He called the

800 number and spoke with a random representative who answered the phone. When asked about the specific details of his collection, he provided all the personal and private details he assumed the representative would need. After all, he *trusted* this company, having been insured with them for several decades.

But what Larry failed to take into consideration is that the representative he talked to didn't know him at all. For all Larry knew, this person could have been hired a week earlier. Now they knew the value of his precious metals collection and *where it was*. Larry regretted his decision. He realized it might have been better to seek out a local specialist, one who could be vouched for, before sharing sensitive information with a complete stranger. By working with a local specialist who has been in business for many years, he gains at least one small advantage—professional reputation. The local business owner may have a lot more to lose than the random employee who answers the telephone.

Pillar #2: Experience, not age

A factory had a major problem that closed their manufacturing line. A consultant was hired to identify the problem and find a solution. After poking around for a few hours, he took out a small hammer and tapped a few times on a particular piece of machinery. The factory line came back to life and production resumed.

A week later, the factory received an invoice for $10,000 from the consultant for the work performed. The factory's owner was upset over the price for less than one day of work and asked for an itemized invoice.

A short time later the second invoice arrived. The invoice listed two items. Item #1 was, "Rectifying problem with hammer: $100." Item #2 was "Knowing where to use hammer: $9,900."

Let's assume Earl has identified two investment professionals as potential candidates to hire. After he meets with them, he discovers one is 45 years old and the other 55. His initial inclination may be to hire the 55-year-old because they are closer to his age and he may initially presume they are more knowledgeable and experienced. But as he continues his due diligence process, he discovers the younger professional has 20 years of industry experience while the older has less than a decade of experience.

In the investment industry, investment experience can vary widely from one professional to another. And real experience comes from navigating financial markets as trends change over the years. For instance, the 45-year-old may have navigated clients through two declining stock market trends during his career, where losses exceeded 50 percent from beginning to end. The 55-year-old, in comparison, may have little or no experience with a declining stock market trend since the last one took place before they began their career. Ten years' experience in most industries may seem like a long time but that may not be true in the investment industry.

Some investment professionals are making money for their clients today simply because they are riding the trend. Remember, a rising tide lifts all boats. It's also important not to confuse a rising stock market trend with knowledge or wisdom. Earl might want to ask the following three questions to each investment professional he is considering before he makes a final decision:

1. How many years of experience do you have in the investment industry?

2. After the 2008 stock market decline, what did you learn and take away from that experience? (If they have 20 years of experience or more, you should also ask what they learned from the 2000 to 2002 downturn as well.)

3. What are you doing differently today with your investment strategy to try to prevent a similar outcome in the future?

If either one or both are unable to answer these questions to his satisfaction, Earl might be inclined to keep searching.

Pillar #3: Fees, not contingent deferred sales charges

Optimism and high expectations often accompany a new business partnership. But unfortunately, not all partnerships work out as originally expected and sometimes the partners decide to go separate ways.

One decision Earl did make not long ago was to purchase a variable annuity from his neighbor who was a broker. And if he decides to hire a new investment professional, he wants to consolidate all his investments with that new person. But due to licensing issues, he may not be able to, if for example, he decides to hire a fee-only advisor. In such an event, Earl might have to leave his investments unconsolidated. Or he might have to sell the annuity, which could result in a contingent deferred sales charge (CDSC).

A CDSC occurs when an investor sells a financial product within a certain period from when they made their initial purchase. When Earl purchased his variable annuity, the insurance company paid his broker and brokerage firm a commission, which in his case was 7 percent. So on a $230,000 annuity purchase, the commission paid was approximately $16,100. But if Earl decides to sell the annuity after the free look-back period expires but before the CDSC expires, the insurance company will charge Earl's account to recoup the outstanding balance of the CDSC they paid his broker.

To avoid such a situation, you might consider three options.

First, if you decide to hire a broker and sometime thereafter part ways, you may want to limit new potential candidates to other brokers who hold similar investment licenses and who can consolidate your investments. Second, depending on the reason for the variable annuity recommendation, a fee-only variable annuity may be sufficient, giving you the ability to sell it without a CDSC if your situation changes. Finally, avoid financial products altogether that include a CDSC!

Pillar #4: Use a large, well-known third party custodian

"Chinese wall" is a term used to describe a barrier that prevents the release of sensitive information that, if disclosed, could lead to a conflict of interest. It is more commonly used in investment banks to prevent the disclosure of pending business takeovers in the public sector where some individuals may use that nonpublic information for personal profit. And while this concept applies to business takeovers, I believe you can use it to help protect your money from unscrupulous investment professionals like the Bernie Madoffs of the world.

There are two primary ways to open an investment account with an investment professional. One way is to open an account directly with the firm that employs your investment professional. Examples may include opening an account at firms like Merrill Lynch, Edward Jones, UBS, or Wells Fargo Advisors. A second way is to open an account held away from the firm that employs your investment professional. For instance, you might decide to hire a broker who represents Edward Jones but your investments may be held directly by an issuing company, like the American Funds Company. Or if you hire a fee-only advisor instead, your investments may be held by a company called a third-party custodian. A few of the larger and more well-known companies who offer third-party custodial services include Charles Schwab, TD Ameritrade, Fidelity (including NFS, a division of Fidelity), and Pershing. (In late 2019, it was announced TD Ameritrade is being purchased by Charles Schwab.)

Using accounts that are held by a third-party custodian creates a type of Chinese wall to help prevent fraudulent activity from taking place in your account by your investment professional. This can severely limit, if not eliminate, the modification of your statements or personal documents by someone like Madoff. Since that information would be created and reported by the third-party custodian only, you can rest assured it is accurate and true.

In most cases, this isn't an issue. But if you have a choice, I suggest choosing a method that brings you the most peace of mind. If Bernie Madoff's firm had used one of the above-mentioned custodians, he probably would not have succeeded.

Pillar #5: Use a third-party performance reporting service

A third-party performance reporting service can add a layer of security and protection to your accounts. These companies aggregate the data reported on your statements and provide you with an independent report. The report may include items such as contributions and withdrawals in your account over a specified period, the total fees paid to your investment professional during that period, the dividends and interest paid on your financial investments, and your investment performance before taxes. Examples of third-party performance providers include companies like Albridge, Advyzon, and Orion Advisor.

These services promote full transparency. When all information is laid bare on the table, whether good or bad, it helps build trust between you and your investment professional.

KEY TAKEAWAYS

While it isn't necessary to use all five pillars, the more you use, the less likely you are to experience regret. If you use all five, then I believe you have done everything within your control to establish a mutually beneficial partnership with your investment professional. If, after implementing these pillars, something happens contrary to your expectations, it's okay. You can't prevent everything that can happen.

Mallory only used one of the five pillars. First, she trusted the bank because she did all her personal and business banking with them for many years. But it wasn't the bank that managed her investment account, it was a person. Remember: People, not paper. Second, her broker was not new to the industry, but she lacked experience for how to deal with changing trends.

Third, the mutual funds Mallory purchased contained a one percent CDSC if she decided to sell them within a year. Even if she had the inclination to sell some of her investments as the decline began, this could have caused reluctance to sell them. Fourth, her mutual fund investments were held at one of the previously mentioned third-party custodians, creating a Chinese wall. And fifth, since Mallory's broker fees were not fee-based, but paid through the mutual funds themselves, an independent, third-party performance reporting service would not have been available.

CHAPTER 13

A Different Outcome

Change the changeable;
Accept the unchangeable;
Remove the unacceptable

–Dr. Kevin Elko

WHEN YOU FIRST BEGAN READING THIS BOOK, WHAT were your initial investment beliefs? Did you believe that suffering investment loss in the stock market was simply unavoidable? Did you believe some of these losses were just the price you had to pay when investing in the stock market? If so, I hope you no longer feel that way. Having said that, I am not implying that all investment loss can be avoided. Investment loss will happen from time to time if you choose to invest your wealth in the stock market. As Dr. Elko says, accept the unchangeable.

However, Dr. Elko also says, *remove the unacceptable*. Regardless of your age, phase of life, or personal risk tolerance, losing 42 percent of your investment wealth should be unacceptable to any profit-seeking investor. So if you agree with this, then I suggest you *change the changeable*. To help limit the possibility of repeating Mallory's experience over your future investing years, you might consider three changes, all of which are within your control.

The first change is to avoid investing in the stock market entirely. Your personal circumstances may not require that you invest in the stock market at all.

The second change is to choose a more conservative asset allocation. Mallory invested 90 percent of her money into stock mutual funds and 10 percent in bond mutual funds. Had she been more conservative with her asset allocation, she likely would have lost less. However, her tradeoff may have been lower performance returns to grow her wealth over future years.

The third change is to choose a different investment strategy. Remember, Mallory used a Buy & Substitute strategy, which in her case meant remaining fully invested in her stock investments. Regardless of whether the primary trend of the stock market was rising or declining, the portion of her wealth invested in the stock market was likely to trend in a similar direction.

Since this book began with Mallory, I believe it only fitting to end with her as well. So considering what you have learned in the previous chapters, let's rewrite her story to reflect what could have been, had Mallory been more knowledgeable and made different decisions.

A DIFFERENT OUTCOME

In 2007, Mallory was approached by a consolidation company that wanted to buy her business and within 90 days, terms for a deal were reached. But she wasn't sure what to do next so she deposited the check at her local bank while contemplating her next course of action.

At the bank, the teller suggested meeting with one of their investment professionals in the bank's private client group. Since she had always trusted the bank, she agreed to the meeting. But after a few meetings, she didn't feel as if she had enough information to make an informed decision. So she decided to continue her research.

The more Mallory thought about it, she wondered if she could find her answer in the business she just sold. After all, her business ebbed and flowed based on economic trends. And she had to make annual staffing changes based on seasonal trends. So she began researching investment philosophies that were conceptually similar.

During her research, she discovered a technical analysis philosophy called trend following. She believed this was the closest fit to how she managed her business. She then reflected on her past meetings with the broker at the bank. The broker's recommendation consisted of investing in several actively managed mutual funds from a well-known mutual fund family. Within these mutual funds, her wealth would be invested in many different stocks in different sectors and countries around the world, providing ample diversification.

But Mallory realized by diversifying her money among many investments, she might own some that were in rising trends and others that were in declining trends. As a profit-seeking investor, she wasn't sure that was wise.

She started asking other people how they invested their money. She began with her father, then asked her bookkeeper, CPA, business attorney, and some of her close friends, seeking to gain an understanding for why they chose to invest their money as they did. From these discussions, she learned about several different investment strategies.

When she had previously asked what to expect for future potential investment return, she was told 9 to 10 percent on average, at least over the longer term. But she realized that an average return included both positive and negative performance years. And while smaller negative years might not be problematic, larger ones could. So after researching and carefully evaluating the pros and cons of several different investment strategies, she chose Buy & Sell—not because she wanted her investments traded but because she wanted a strategy that offered the most flexibility to help protect her wealth when future trends change. She hoped her long-term average investment returns might be improved by attempting to limit her investment losses.

Mallory's next step was a little easier. She now needed to seek out, identify, and interview investment professionals who shared a similar philosophy and offered a Buy & Sell strategy. The bank's investment professional was not the right fit for her so she thanked them for their time and focused her attention elsewhere. She next turned to those individuals who could be a right fit out of the network her friends, family, and business professionals were already working with. But she continued to look for others as well.

Based on the amount of Mallory's personal savings and after-tax sale proceeds, she decided she only needed one investment professional for her needs at that time. So after narrowing down her candidates, she decided to hire the investment professional who she felt had financial interests aligned with hers. In addition, there were some other aspects that helped instill a sense of confidence in her decision. They had experience. The investments they recommended did not provide them with any compensation. Her investments were held at a firm that was unrelated to their advisory firm. And she would receive independent, quarterly performance reports to help her stay abreast of her progress.

Mallory decided on a growth-oriented investment plan hoping to maximize her long-term investment returns. She asked her new investment professional to walk her through any potential embedded tax issues on the investments she was about to purchase since she had just paid a hefty tax bill from the sale of her business. With her questions answered satisfactorily, Mallory and her investment professional discussed how to invest her money in the financial markets. Because the trend was rising at that time, they decided to use a dollar-cost-averaging strategy and to invest her money over several months.

Over the next calendar year, the unthinkable happened. The trend of the stock market changed and stock prices declined significantly. Having invested 90 percent of her money into stock investments and 10 percent into bond investments, what might her account statement reflect for the value of her account? Without accounting for potential changes in the value of her bond investments, her risk-managed stock investments could have declined by approximately 14 percent.[23]

While Mallory may not have been pleased with her absolute return, she may have been pleased with her relative return. By limiting her investment loss, she might be able to recover her investment value in less time compared to other investment strategies.

Once again, this story is not suggesting what is *probable*, simply what is *possible*, depending on your choices and the financial market trends that play out during your investment lifetime. And even though this story is completely hypothetical, I must remind you that past performance is not indicative of future results.

AFTERWORD

Thirteen years have passed since the day Mallory sold her business, and in 12 of those 13 years the United States stock market has enjoyed a rising trend. Chart X illustrates what I believe is a rising primary trend through the end of calendar year 2019.

CHART X

Chart courtesy of Stockcharts.com

Based on my interpretation of historical trends, the longest unimpeded rising stock market trend in the United States began in 1983 and ended in 2000, lasting 17 years. So unless the current rising trend sets a record (which it may), the potential for a trend correction increases with each passing day.

Two phrases I like to keep in mind in life are "What if?" and "If only." When it pertains to the financial markets, your financial wealth, and your long-term financial well-being, I hope after reading this book you will prepare diligently for the former and not have to reflect one day on the latter. Again, while there is no single strategy that will perform perfectly all the time, there are some that could perform better than others, depending on the prevailing primary trend.

I hope the information and concepts presented in this book help you assess your current choice of investment strategy to be prepared for whatever trends the future brings.

References

Chart 1A

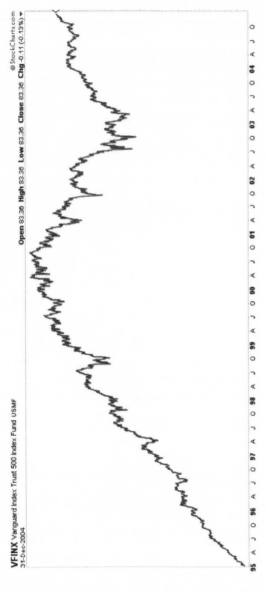

Chart courtesy of Stockcharts.com

Chart 1B

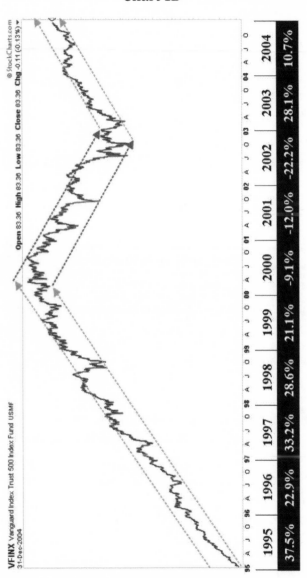

Chart courtesy of Stockcharts.com

Chart 1C

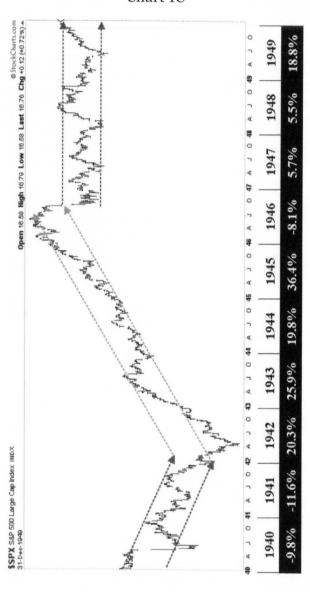

Chart courtesy of Stockcharts.com

Chart 1D

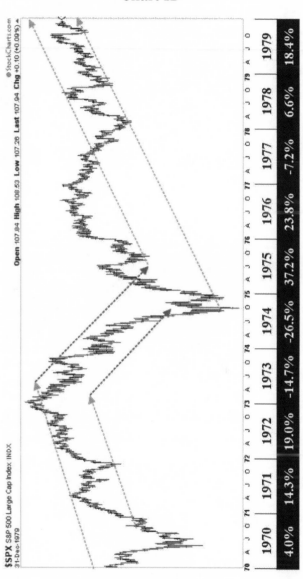

Chart courtesy of Stockcharts.com

Chart 1E

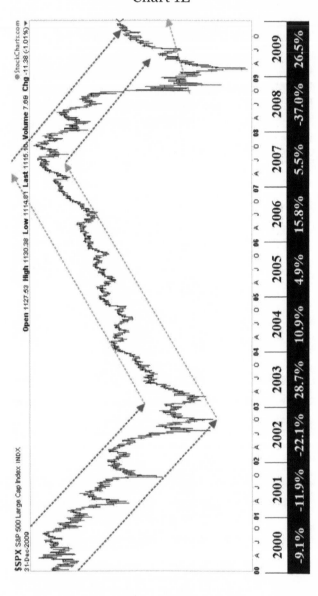

Chart courtesy of Stockcharts.com

Table 3A

1990	1991	1992	1993	1994	1995	1996	1997	1998	1999
-3.1%	30.5%	7.6%	10.1%	1.3%	37.6%	23.0%	33.4%	28.6%	21.0%

2000	2001	2002	2003	2004	2005	2006	2007	2008	2009
-9.1%	-11.9%	-22.1%	28.7%	10.9%	4.9%	15.8%	5.5%	-37.0%	26.5%

Table 4A

STRATEGY	1995	1996	1997	1998	1999
S&P 500 Index	37.6%	23.0%	33.4%	28.6%	21.0%
BUY & HOLD	37.5%	22.9%	33.2%	28.6%	21.1%
BUY & SUBSTITUTE	29.8%	14.8%	26.9%	31.8%	45.7%
BUY & SELL	11.0%	10.5%	12.4%	12.3%	13.0%

Table 4C

STRATEGY	2008
S&P 500 Index	-37.0%
BUY & HOLD	-37.0%
BUY & SUBSTITUTE	-39.1%
BUY & SELL	-13.9%

Protecting the Pig

Table 4D

STRATEGY	2000 (Y1)	2001 (Y2)	2002 (Y3)	2003 (Y4)	2004 (Y5)	2005 (Y6)	2006 (Y7)
S&P 500 Index	$ 90.94	$ 80.01	$ 62.29	$ 80.04	$ 88.63	$ 92.86	$ 107.39
BUY & HOLD	$ 90.94	$ 80.01	$ 62.29	$ 80.04	$ 88.63	$ 92.86	$ 107.39
BUY & SUBSTITUTE	$ 107.49	$ 94.71	$ 73.85	$ 97.54	$ 109.20	$ 124.75	$ 144.44
BUY & SELL	$ 106.61	$ 102.85	$ 97.85	$ 109.21	$ 116.80	$ 122.25	$ 134.64

Table 4E

STRATEGY	2008 (Y1)	2009 (Y2)	2010 (Y3)	2011 (Y4)	2012 (Y5)
S&P 500 Index	$ 62.98	$ 79.66	$ 91.54	$ 93.34	$108.11
BUY & HOLD	$ 62.98	$ 79.66	$ 91.54	$ 93.34	$108.11
BUY & SUBSTITUTE	$ 60.93	$ 81.94	$ 92.00	$ 87.50	$105.47
BUY & SELL	$ 86.08	$ 91.74	$ 96.17	$ 99.04	$103.51
BUY & SELL [8],[9]	$ 85.80	$126.38	$149.13	$144.51	$168.35

Table 4F

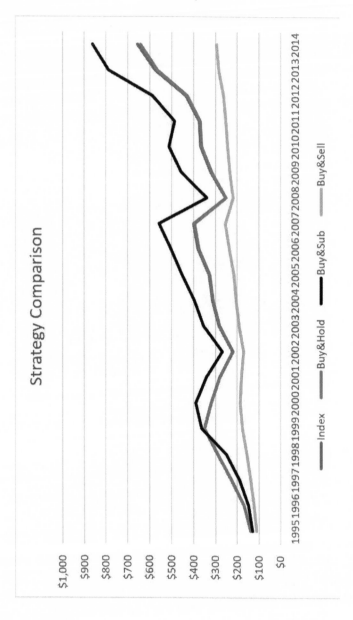

Chart 5A

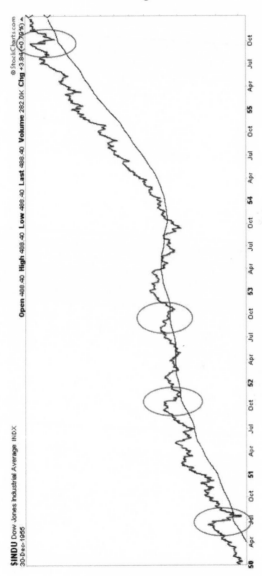

Chart courtesy of Stockcharts.com

Chart 5B

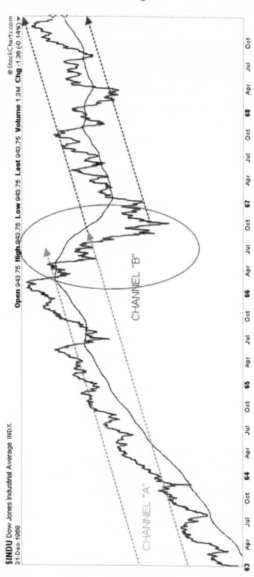

Chart courtesy of Stockcharts.com

Chart 5C

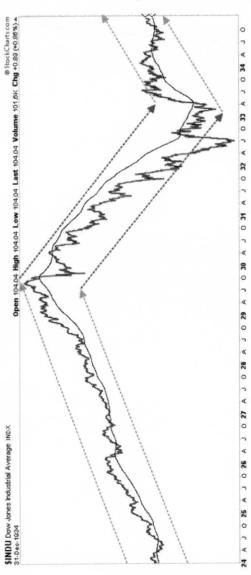

Chart courtesy of Stockcharts.com

Table 5A

Digging A Hole

Small losses are easier to recover from, compared with big drops

Initial loss	Gain needed to recover
8%	8.7%
25	33
30	43
40	67
50	100

Table 5B

STRATEGY	2008	2009
S&P 500 Index	-37.0%	26.5%
BUY & HOLD	-37.0%	26.5%
BUY & SUBSTITUTE	-39.1%	34.5%
BUY & SELL	-13.9%	6.6%

Chart 6A

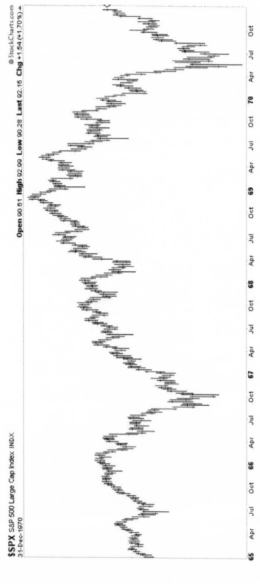

Chart courtesy of Stockcharts.com

Chart 6B

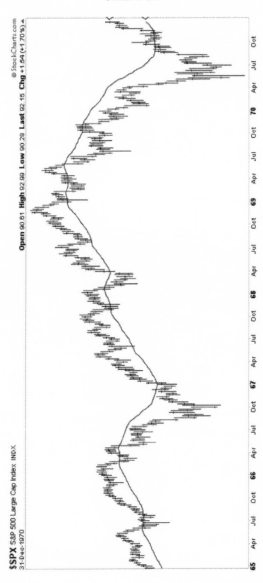

Chart courtesy of Stockcharts.com

Chart 6C

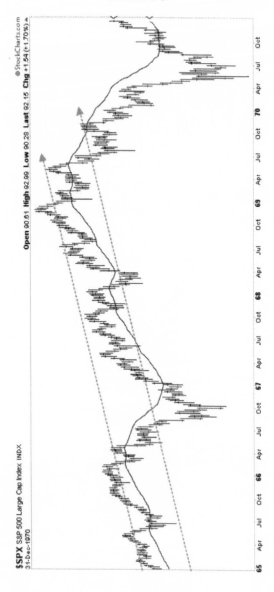

Chart courtesy of Stockcharts.com

Chart 6D

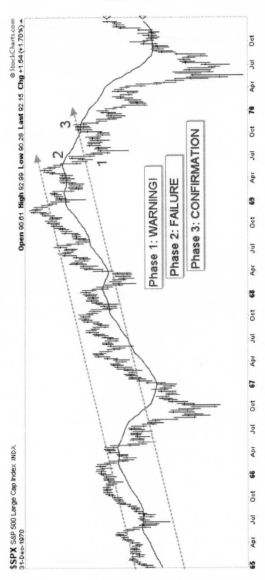

Chart courtesy of Stockcharts.com

Chart 6E

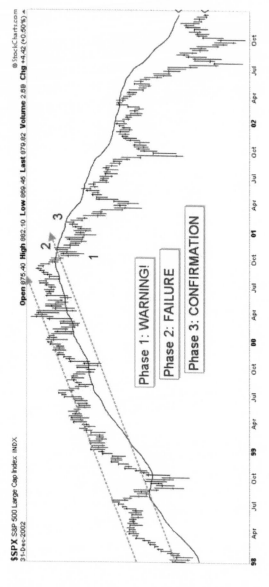

Chart courtesy of Stockcharts.com

Chart 6F

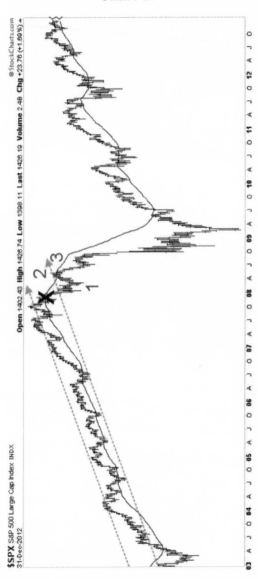

Chart courtesy of Stockcharts.com

Chart 7A

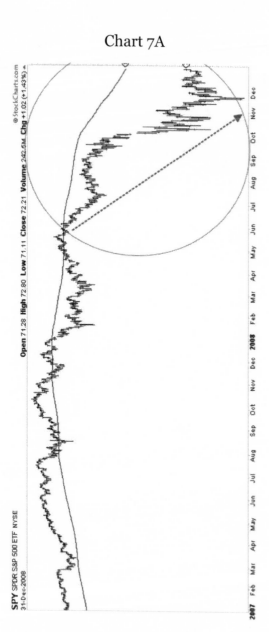

Chart courtesy of Stockcharts.com

Chart 7B

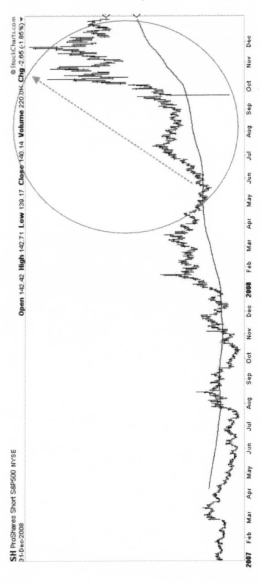

Chart courtesy of Stockcharts.com

Chart 7C

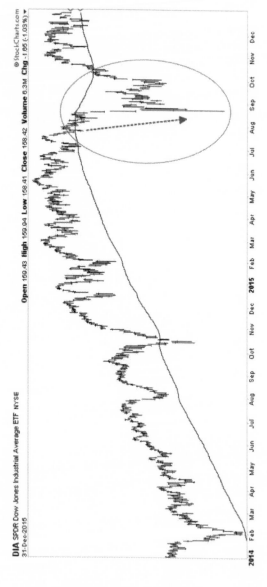

Chart courtesy of Stockcharts.com

Chart 7D

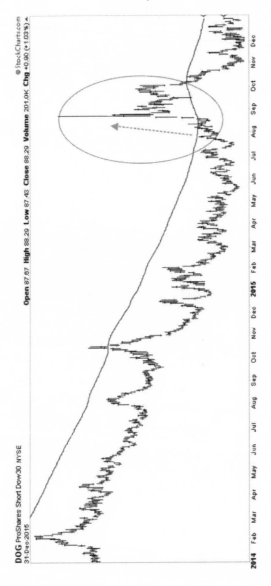

Chart courtesy of Stockcharts.com

Table 9A

INVESTMENT:	SYMBOL:	ALLOCATION:
BUCKET 1: "Stable value investments"		
Guggenheim Limited Duration Fund	GILHX	3.3%
Guggenheim High Yield Fund	SHYIX	3.3%
Nuveen Managed Muni Portfolio	N/A	8.9%
Vanguard Wellesley Income	VWINX	4.4%
BUCKET 2: "Alternative income sources"		
Nationwide Immediate Income Annuity	N/A	11.1%
Blackstone real estate investment	N/A	4.4%
Structured product	N/A	4.4%
BUCKET 3: "Growth-biased investments"		
Alger Small Cap Focus	AOFYX	2.2%
American Funds Capital Income Builder	CAIFX	4.4%
Boston Partners All Cap Value	BPAIX	6.7%
Chiron Capital Allocation	CCAPX	6.7%
First Eagle Global	SGIIX	4.4%
Guggenheim Total Return Bond	GIBIX	4.4%
JP Morgan Income Builder	JNBSX	4.4%
Western Asset Core Plus Bond	WACPX	4.4%
CIO High Quality Dividend Yield Portfolio	N/A	22.2%

Chart 10A

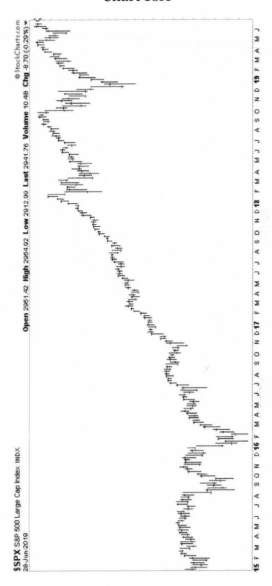

Chart courtesy of Stockcharts.com

Chart 10B

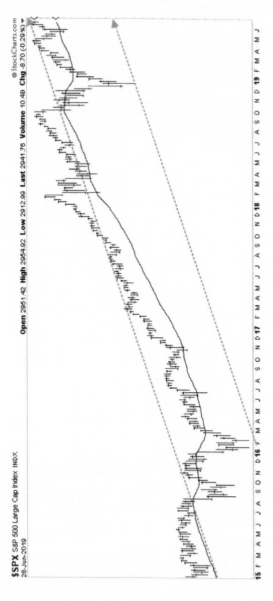

Chart courtesy of Stockcharts.com

Endnotes

1   www.nameberry.com/babyname/Mallory

2   www.investopedia.com/terms/m/movingaverage.asp

3   www.slickcharts.com/sp500/returns

4   The Buy & Hold strategy is represented by The Vanguard 500 Index Fund (symbol VFINX).

5   The Buy & Substitute strategy is represented by the Growth Fund of America (symbol AGTHX).

6   The Buy & Sell strategy is represented by the Gateway Fund (symbol GATEX).

7   The Gateway Fund buys put options to manage stock market risk, which differs from a "buy low, sell high" strategy. However, it is a risk-managed strategy nonetheless with a performance record during this historical period. As such, I believe it to be an appropriate investment for purposes of this lesson.

8   The Bluestone Elite strategy is another type of risk-managed strategy. Additional information can be found at www.bluestonecm.com.

9   The Bluestone Elite strategy's inception date was October 2003.

10 The S&P 500 Index is one of the most commonly followed equity indices, and many consider it one of the best representations of the US stock market, and a bellwether for the US. economy. It is comprised of 500 large companies having common stock listed on the NYSE or NASDAQ. It is not possible to invest directly in this index.

11 https://www.investors.com/how-to-invest-investors-corner-still-the-1-rule-for-stock-investors-always-cut-your-losses-short/

12 The Dow Jones Industrial Average (DJIA) is an index that tracks 30 large, publicly-owned blue chip companies trading on the New York Stock Exchange (NYSE) and the NASDAQ.

13 Investopedia.com/terms/i/inverse-etf.asp

14 A certificate of deposit, or CD, is a product offered by banks and credit unions that provides an interest rate premium in exchange for the customer agreeing to leave a lump-sum deposit untouched for a predetermined period of time.

15 Earl's previously purchased financial investments consist of C-share mutual funds that do not currently have any contingent deferred sales charges remaining. Further, potential tax repercussions from selling them are almost nonexistent. Therefore, for purposes of this chapter, there appears to be little reason not to combine all under a tiered asset management fee to save him money.

16 This is not to say that Mallory would not have suffered loss if she used any other strategy. It is simply to point out that a Buy & Hold strategy is simply that—you buy, then you hold.

17 www.finra.org/media-center/statistics#key

18 www.statista.com/statistics/614815/number-of-rias-employed-usa/

19 www.wsj.com/articles/SB110356207980304862

20 A Ponzi scheme, according to Investopedia.com, is a fraudulent investing scam promising high rates of return with little risk to investors.

21 E.g., David Bell, *Regret in Decision Making Under Uncertainty*, 30 OPERATIONS RES. 961, 961 (1982); Thomas Gilovich & Victoria Husted Medvec, The Experience of Regret: What, When, and Why, 102 PSYCHOL. REV. 379, 379 (1995); Graham Loomes & Robert Sugden, *Regret Theory: An Alternative Theory of Rational Choice Under Uncertainty*, 92 ECON. J. 805, 805 (1982); Marcel Zeelenberg et al., *Consequences of Regret Aversion: Effects of Expected Feedback on Risky Decision Making*, 65 ORG. BEHAV. & HUM. PROCESSES 148, 150 (1996) [hereinafter Zeelenberg et al., *Consequences*]; The terms "risk" and "uncertainty" are often used interchangeably, but classical economics defines each in a slightly different manner. Under risk, the probability of an outcome is not certain but is knowable, while uncertainty describes the circumstance where the probabilities are not only indeterminate but also unknown to the actor. Carol A. Heimer, *Social Structure, Psychology, and the Estimation of Risk*, 14 ANN. REV. Soc. 491, 493 (1998).

22 Loomes & Sugden, *supra* note 1, at 808.

23 Past performance is not indicative of future results. The performance referenced here is simply reproducing the average performance for the Buy & Sell investment strategies introduced in Chapter 4 during calendar year 2008.

Made in the USA
Middletown, DE
11 April 2021

37361512R00111